One life. Pure and simple.

Christianity Explored Universal Leader's Guide (2nd Edition)
Copyright © 2012 Christianity Explored / The Good Book Company
www.ceministries.org

Published by
The Good Book Company Ltd
Tel (UK): 0333-123-0880
Tel (International): +44 (0) 208 942 0880
Email: admin@thegoodbook.co.uk

Websites:
UK: www.thegoodbook.co.uk
N America: www.thegoodbook.com
Australia: www.thegoodbook.com.au
New Zealand: www.thegoodbook.co.nz

ISBN: 9781908317872

Design by Steve Devane and André Parker

Printed in China

Introduction

Welcome to the Universal Edition of *Christianity Explored*.

This eight-session course of Bible study and discussion aims to introduce people to Jesus Christ through Mark's Gospel, in an environment where they are free to ask any questions they like.

What makes this course – and the Christian gospel – distinctive is its insistence on God's remarkable grace: the clear teaching that although we have rebelled against God, we are deeply loved by him. Loved with an outrageous, costly and incomprehensible love that was poured out for us on a little hill just outside Jerusalem.

This second edition has been reworked from the previous "English made easy" edition. Over a series of eight Bible studies and discussions, group members will discover the identity, mission and call of Jesus – who Jesus is, what he came to do, and how he calls us to respond.

This Universal Edition is written with a concern to make the language crystal clear and accessible to the widest range of potential users throughout the world. Many of the words in the Bible are complex and difficult to understand for those who have been believers a long time, let alone those who are just taking their first tentative steps. So these studies are designed to be suitable for a wide variety of groups, including those for whom English is a second language.

This Leader's Guide is divided into two sections. The first will train you to use the course, and the second will be your guide each week as you lead the studies, giving answers, background and other helpful information to encourage you as you lead your group through Mark.

If you are running a *Christianity Explored Universal* course, please register it on our website **www.ceministries.org**, so that we and others can pray for you, or even send other people along.

May God richly bless you in all you do with this course for the honour and glory of Christ.

The Christianity Explored Team, March 2012

Section 1: How to run the course 7

Section 2: Study guide 45

Appendices 117

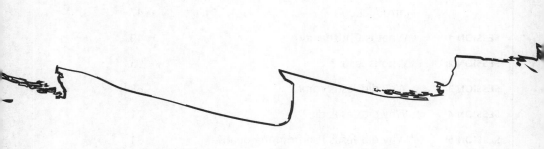

How to run the course

Two *Christianity Explored* websites to help you:

www.christianityexplored.org
This website is for non-Christians, whether or not they are on a course. It features a visual gospel outline based on the Gospel of Mark, answers to common questions, and testimonies from a wide variety of people, as well as information about the *Christianity Explored* course. You can find more details at the back of this book, on page 143.

www.ceministries.org
For leaders looking for information, downloads and resources.

Getting started

Telling people about Jesus Christ is a stunning privilege and a huge responsibility. It's a stunning privilege because Almighty God is pleased to call us his "fellow workers" (1 Corinthians 3:9) as he seeks and saves the lost. And it's a huge responsibility because it can be tempting to present a watered-down gospel that has no power to save and is "no gospel at all" (Galatians 1:7). Our evangelism must always be careful, prayerful and faithful.

Christianity Explored Universal has been developed to let the gospel tell the gospel. It takes your group members on an eight-session journey through Mark's Gospel to discover who Jesus is, why he came and what it means to follow him.

You may be someone who usually skips introductions, but can we please encourage you to read through these notes carefully. They will help your journey run smoothly.

WHO WILL COME?

Christianity Explored Universal is a course that helps people discover the life of Jesus together. It doesn't make assumptions about knowledge of the Bible or any religious background people may have. The course uses simple, clear English, which makes it ideal for those who have English as a second language as well as anyone who will appreciate crystal-clear language. It will also suit any group that prefers to take a Bible-study approach to exploring Christianity.

Because the course involves discussion, it is best to limit the size of a group to a maximum of 12 (6-8 if you are working with internationals). More than this, and the quieter people in the group will not feel able to participate. It may be best to have separate groups for those with English as a second language, as this will allow everyone to go at a pace they are comfortable with – but don't worry if this is not possible.

HOW WILL I INVITE THEM?

Advertise the course in your church bulletin, during the Sunday services and at events you run for internationals. Explain who the course is for, and what will happen at it.

You may want to organize a guest event such as a sports afternoon, a Christmas carol service, a campus mission, a picnic and so on. At the end of the event, give an invitation to join *Christianity Explored*.

Tell people that it is an opportunity to be part of a group that will discuss parts of the Bible together to explore the life of Jesus. There will also be plenty of opportunities to ask any questions they like. Reassure people that no one will be expected to pray, sing or do anything that will make them feel embarrassed.

People are often more likely to join a group if they are invited personally. You can make your own invitations and posters using downloadable logos (available at www.ceministries.org).

WHERE WILL WE MEET?

Try to find a place where you will be able to meet every week at the same time. The important thing is that the environment should help people relax so that they will be encouraged to discuss freely. Sharing a meal together will help with this.

Comfortable church premises provide a neutral meeting ground that is also free of distraction.

Homes are another option, but be aware that some may not be used to visiting other people's homes. Alternatively, some groups may meet in a hired room. Be careful of choosing a place that is too exposed to the public, where there can be many distractions or people may feel embarrassed.

WHEN WILL WE MEET?

It's important to meet as regularly as possible. Most groups meet once a week on a midweek evening. However, your group and situation may be different. Eg:

- a daytime women's group

- a fortnightly home group

- a church houseparty

- a Sunday group running at the same time as the regular church service

- a college Christian Union or fellowship

- a few people meeting round a kitchen table

The course material can be adapted to suit your situation, including meeting one-to-one with a friend or neighbour. However, you will find it helpful to meet as regularly as possible – and please don't skip any sessions or change the order. You should be able to complete each study in 1½ to 2 hours, depending on the ability of the group.

Choose the time to suit the particular group of people you are aiming at. Often Christians can get into a rut when planning meetings. We may have become used to meetings that start at 7.30pm and end by 9.30pm. That may or may not be the best time for the guests. Have you considered that lunchtime may be best for some kinds of groups, or even early morning, mid morning or afternoon? Be imaginative but realistic about the people being invited, and ask them what might suit them best.

You may also want to spend time with the participants outside of the course in order to have the time to deal effectively with issues that come up during the studies. Time spent with individuals is also the quickest way to develop a trusting relationship.

A caution: it is completely inappropriate to be meeting up one-to-one with members of the opposite sex. There may also be important cultural differences that you are unaware of if you are meeting with someone from another country. See the section on Cross Cultural Evangelism on page 33 for more about this.

WHO WILL LEAD?

Ideally, you should have two leaders for every six participants. The leaders are responsible for guiding the studies and discussion. In a mixed group, it is desirable to have both a male and a female leader so that they can deal with pastoral situations appropriately.

Leaders should be Christians who are able to teach, encourage discussion and care for participants. They should be able to teach the Bible faithfully and clearly, and handle pastoral situations with care and sensitivity.

WHAT WILL WE NEED?

- **Food.** If you are able to share a meal together, it will make the whole experience better. On a practical level, people will talk and participate more if they spend more time together, and they will open up to you as the leader more as they spend more time with you. If it is impractical to serve a meal, provide light refreshments (coffee and cake, for example).

Bibles. Everyone on the course – leaders and participants – will need a Bible. There are downloadable sheets of the relevant passages from Mark in the NIV version available at www.ceministries.org, or you can download and print out other versions of the Bible, including foreign-language versions (from www. biblegateway.com).

For the sake of clarity, it is important that everyone uses the same version. (The version used throughout the course material is the New International Version.) If they do not already have one, participants should be given a Mark's Gospel or Bible at the start of the course, preferably one they can take away with them. In many cases it will also be essential to provide participants with a copy of the Bible in their own language. Go to www.ceministries.org for information on locating Bibles.

Handbook. Make sure you have enough copies of the Handbook so that every group member has their own copy. Provide pens as well.

DVD. It is not essential to use the DVD for the Universal edition of *Christianity Explored*, but you may find it useful to show it as a kind of summary at the end of the study. Certainly, watching the programmes yourself will increase your understanding of Mark's Gospel, and help you to explain it more clearly to your group.

Preparing yourself and your co-leaders

A well-prepared *Christianity Explored* leader will be committed in three particular areas:

1. Committed to the Bible

2. Committed to prayer

3. Committed to people

1. COMMITTED TO THE BIBLE

The Bible is God's word. Whenever we open the Bible, God speaks to us. In Hebrews 4:12 we read: "For the word of God is living and active. Sharper than any double-edged sword, it penetrates even to dividing soul and spirit, joints and marrow; it judges the thoughts and attitudes of the heart." Nothing else can do this.

God's word is where the power is. Whatever his personal circumstances, Paul knew that if the word were preached, it would do its work: "I am suffering even to the point of being chained like a criminal. But God's word is not chained" (2 Timothy 2:9).

In 2 Timothy 2:15, Paul urges Timothy to devote himself to the study of God's word: "Do your best to present yourself to God as one approved, a workman who does not need to be ashamed and who correctly handles the word of truth."

Because we're convinced of the power of God's word, every group member should be given a Mark's Gospel or Bible of their own at the beginning of the course – and our focus as leaders should consistently be on the Bible, specifically Mark's Gospel.

■ **Read Mark's Gospel all the way through** – not just the passages that will be looked at during the course. It is vital that you study Mark for yourself and think about its application in your own life. If the message of Mark doesn't excite you, it won't be exciting for those who attend the course.

■ **Think about each passage from your group member's point of view.** What might they not understand? What questions and problems might come to their mind? (You will find a list of common questions from Mark's Gospel on page 125.) Which words will you have to explain to people learning English? (There are word lists for each session in both the Handbook and this Leader's Guide.)

■ **Think about different ways of explaining things.** Although this is a Bible study, some people think visually, so you might want to get a whiteboard or a large sheet of paper to write on. This is also useful for writing up new words (for those learning English). You may be able to think of some diagrams / illustrations which will help people to understand an important point.

■ **Know the course material.** Go through the questions in the Handbook and read the notes in this Leader's Guide. This will help you to be clear where each session is heading so that you can guide the group through it.

2. COMMITTED TO PRAYER

Prayer is essential before, during and after the course. Paul opens his letter to Timothy by saying: "Night and day I constantly remember you in my prayers" (2 Timothy 1:3). We, too, need to be constantly remembering the guests and our fellow leaders in our prayers.

Being dedicated to the Bible and prayer means being single-minded. As 2 Timothy 2:4 says: "No-one serving as a soldier gets involved in civilian affairs – he wants to please his commanding officer". Because the work of evangelism is so important, we must be ruthless in organizing our schedules to that end. The course will have a huge impact on our time.

Again and again, as we seek to make time to lead, to study Mark, to pray and to meet up with group members, the good will be the enemy of the best, and the urgent will be the enemy of the important. We may find temptations or feelings of inadequacy creeping in. Sometimes, leading will be a real struggle: physically, emotionally and spiritually. After all, our enemy Satan hates the work we are doing.

But as Paul's illustration of the soldier makes clear, we must remain dedicated. If people stop attending, we keep praying for them. If they don't seem interested in the discussions, we keep studying and teaching Mark. We must not be discouraged, because we do it all for our "commanding officer", the Lord Jesus Christ.

One of the main reasons why we don't pray is that we don't plan to pray. As you set aside time to prepare for your *Christianity Explored* group, include time for praying for the other leaders, hosts and guests.

■ **If you are a lone leader** – then ask someone else to pray with you each week.

■ **If there are a number of leaders** – then meet up and pray.

14

- **Why not organise a prayer group?** Recruit people from your church to pray for you as you meet together with your group for each session.

- **And remember to pray yourself.** Keep a list of the people who come, other leaders and even other groups. Put the list where you will see it daily (in your Bible?) and pray for them.

- **Use the word of God to pray** – this helps avoid mental drift and ensures biblical praying. It allows God to set the agenda for your prayers. Pray for people along the lines of the main point of each session.

- **Pray specifically and expectantly.** God loves to answer prayers, and, if you pray for specific things to happen, and for particular problems to be resolved, you will be encouraged as you see God answering.

3. COMMITTED TO PEOPLE

God's plan is for the gospel to be communicated life to life. It is not just a matter of us delivering a series of arguments or ideas, brain to brain. We must be prepared to share our lives with this group, and to love them for the sake of Christ. Paul shows us the way in 1 Thessalonians 2:8:

> *"We loved you so much that we were delighted to share with you not only the gospel of God but our lives as well, because you had become so dear to us."*

We are not the gospel (Jesus is), but our lives should make the teaching about God our Saviour attractive (see Titus 2:10).

And that means that we need to show genuine concern for people's lives, their struggles and their questions – and not dismiss them as irrelevant. It means we need to respect them, even when they disagree with us. It means we need to open up our own lives to their inspection, and talk about our own weaknesses and failures, as well as the ways that Christ has changed us. Such genuine love and honesty are the marks of a true disciple of Christ, and in and of themselves they can be a compelling answer to many of the doubts that people have.

Guard against the *Christianity Explored* course being perceived in your church* as the interest and responsibility only of those who are directly involved. The care of our guests on *Christianity Explored* needs to be a matter for the whole church family. Only a comparatively few will be actually running the course. But everyone should take ownership of the project as they pray, invite friends, keep up to date with how the course is going and are ready to welcome and share the on-going care of the guests. This will help to spread the excitement of evangelism, and will be a great encouragement to the whole church family.

But love is never without cost. It will involve us in the complex and messy lives that people have. We must understand that mission means mess. It may require us to offer someone practical help. We should do this willingly, but wisely and prayer-fully, and in consultation with other Christians. But don't shrink back because of the cost.

* If you are running *Christianity Explored* as part of a college Christian Fellowship or other non-church group, the above still applies. Every Christian in your group should be prayerfully supporting the course, inviting friends, and welcoming guests when the opportunity arises.

Introducing Mark's Gospel

As a leader preparing to teach Mark, there's no substitute for reading through his Gospel at least two or three times.

And as you read, you'll begin to see three great themes in Mark:

◼ Who is Jesus? (Jesus' *identity*)

◼ Why did he come? (Jesus' *mission*)

◼ What does it mean to follow him? (Jesus' *call*)

Every passage in Mark has something to say to us about one or more of these themes – and the backdrop which creates such drama in Mark is his interest in people's spiritual *blindness* to these issues.

IDENTITY: WHO IS JESUS?

Mark 8 is the chapter on which the book hinges. Beginning in Mark 8:27 we find all three of these themes – identity, mission and call – in quick succession. Before that, Mark sets the scene in Mark 8:22-26 with the unusual healing of a blind man. In the healing process the blind man moves from seeing *nothing* to seeing *something*, then to seeing *everything*.

It seems that Mark records the miracle at this point to help his readers see that the disciples are going through a similar process as their *spiritual blindness* is being overcome.

Let's take a few verses at a time.

👁 **Read Mark 8:27-30**

The dominant question in verses 27-30 is Jesus' *identity*. Who exactly is Jesus?

People had lots of theories, just as they do now: "Some say John the Baptist; others say Elijah; and still others, one of the prophets" (Mark 8:28). They put Jesus in the category of a man sent from God. But actually they are still blind to his true identity. He is not another prophet. He is the one to whom all the prophets pointed.

But Jesus gets very personal in verse 29: "What about you? ... Who do you say I am?"

This is like a mid-term examination for the disciples. There had been lots of debate about the identity of Jesus, and they had seen plenty of evidence pointing to the answer Peter gives here, that Jesus is God's chosen and promised King.

The book of Isaiah talks about the coming of the Christ, God's chosen King:

> "Be strong, do not fear; your God will come, he will come with vengeance; with divine retribution he will come to save you.
>
> Then will the eyes of the blind be opened and the ears of the deaf unstopped. Then will the lame leap like a deer, and the mute tongue shout for joy" (Isaiah 35:4-6).

Through the prophet Isaiah, God told his people how they would recognize the Christ, his promised King, when he came: the deaf will hear, the blind will see, the lame will walk, and the mute will speak.

Among many other miracles recorded in the first half of Mark's Gospel, Jesus makes a lame man walk in chapter 2, he makes a deaf and mute man hear and speak in chapter 7, and he cures a blind man in chapter 8. Jesus demonstrates his power in this specific way so that people will recognize him as the Christ.

👁 **Read Mark 1:2-3**

The second half of the quotation (verse 3) is from Isaiah 40 – a passage that makes it clear that this "Lord" who is mentioned is the creator of the world, the one who miraculously delivered his people from Egypt. Mark tells us that John the Baptist is the "voice of one calling in the desert" who will prepare the way for the Lord. When John baptizes Jesus, the voice from heaven confirms that Jesus is indeed the unique Son of God, the promised Lord of Isaiah 40 (Mark 1:11).

However, despite seeing and hearing Jesus in action, there was much discussion (see Mark 1:27; 2:7, 10-12, 23-28; 4:41; 5:35-42; 6:1-3; 8:14-21). It might seem as if the disciples were never going to get the issue of Jesus' identity right. But Mark inserts the healing of the blind man to signal to us that a miracle is taking place. The disciple's spiritually blind eyes are being opened to see the true identity of Jesus. Peter answers the question concerning Jesus' identity correctly: "You are the Christ".

But is Peter now seeing everything clearly?

MISSION: WHY DID JESUS COME?

So far in Mark we have been given clear indications of the *mission* of Jesus. For example, he gave priority to preaching over healing (Mark 1:35-39), and to spiritual

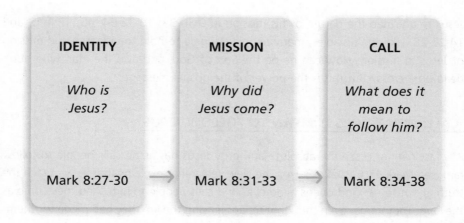

IDENTITY	MISSION	CALL
Who is Jesus?	*Why did Jesus come?*	*What does it mean to follow him?*
Mark 8:27-30	Mark 8:31-33	Mark 8:34-38

health over physical health (Mark 2:5). His choice of company raised questions, but Jesus shows that this is deliberate policy (Mark 2:15-17). This is his mission, to preach the good news, and call sinners. But how can sinners be accepted by God?

👁 **Read Mark 8:31-33**

Here, for the first time, Jesus begins to teach that he "must suffer many things and be rejected by the elders, chief priests and teachers of the law, and that he must be killed and after three days rise again". This is why he has come.

Jesus leaves no room for misunderstanding – he speaks "plainly about this" (verse 32) – because this is his mission and he knows that the disciples, and most of the public, have a very different idea of what the Christ will be like. Their idea is of a triumphant king, marching in to claim his territory, trampling the enemy underfoot, and ushering in a glorious new era for his followers. A Christ who was going to suffer and die would have seemed like a contradiction in terms.

In chapter 8, although Peter has Jesus' *identity* right, it's clear he hasn't yet understood Jesus' *mission*. He has this triumphal view of the Christ in mind when he takes Jesus aside and begins "to rebuke him" (Mark 8:32). But Jesus' strong reaction shows just how necessary death is to his mission: "Get behind me, Satan! ... You do not have in mind the things of God, but the things of men" (Mark 8:33).

Jesus clearly knew that Peter's failure to understand his mission was a result of Satan blinding Peter to it. The idea that the Son of God had to suffer and die is still a stumbling block for many people today. But if we're to understand correctly Mark's Gospel – and indeed the whole Bible – it is essential to grasp the true nature of Jesus' mission: he "must suffer" and "he must be killed" (Mark 8:31) so that we can be forgiven. And we must see that this is one of the "things of God" that Peter did not have in mind.

Jesus re-affirmed the nature of his mission in 9:30-32; 10:32-34, 45; 12:1-12 and 14:27-28. Like the disciples, many people struggle to hold the identity and mission of Jesus in tension. How can he be the Son of God, and also the man who hung dead on a cross? But this is the power of the gospel message.

CALL: WHAT DOES IT MEAN TO FOLLOW JESUS?

It is fascinating to see the absolute authority Jesus has as he calls people to follow him (see Mark 1:16-20; 2:13-14). The New Testament explains that as we teach the truth about Jesus, God opens blind eyes and calls people to him. And they come as they are. They come, even though it means leaving the life they had made for themselves. They come, because they now see that Jesus, and the salvation he offers, is the ultimate treasure.

👁 **Read Mark 8:34-38**

Jesus is very candid about the implications of being his follower. Having just spoken to the disciples about his own death, Jesus calls the crowd to him and says: "If anyone would come after me, he must deny himself and take up his cross and follow me". It is striking to see Jesus immediately turn his attention from the cross *he* must take up, to the cross *we* must take up.

If we are to follow him, Jesus tells us we must deny ourselves. It is not a natural thing for human beings to turn away from self-centredness and self-reliance, but that is Jesus' call. Following him means giving the throne of our lives to him.

And we cannot follow Jesus if we do not take up our cross. The cross was the ultimate sign of humanity's rejection of Jesus. (See Mark 12:1-12, especially verses 7 and 10). Jesus makes it plain that those who follow him will face rejection in this world, where he is still disowned.

Why would anyone be willing to deny themselves, and take up their cross, as they follow Jesus? The answer is that belonging to him is the only way to be saved. If that seems irrational, we need to hear what Jesus says next:

> *"For whoever wants to save his life will lose it, but whoever loses his life for me and for the gospel will save it" (Mark 8:35).*

It sounds like the complete opposite of what we would instinctively think. We would naturally prefer to stay in control of our lives, and to avoid the rejection of friends, family and colleagues that comes from being Jesus' followers. But that will mean we walk away from Jesus – the only one who is able to save us.

Just in case we think that following Jesus sounds like a bad deal, verses 35-38 of chapter 8 give us four very good reasons to follow him:

- If we give up our life for him, we'll save it; and if we don't, we'll lose it (8:35).

- If, by rejecting Jesus, we gain the whole world, we still lose the most important thing we have (8:36).

- If we miss out on eternal life, there's nothing we can do to buy it back (8:37).

- If we reject Jesus, then he will reject us when he returns as Judge of the world (8:38).

This will be a tough world to live in as a follower of Christ. Jesus does not downplay that reality. And as we share the good news with people, we must be prepared to tell them what it means to follow Jesus now. But if they have heard his call, they will come, even though it means substantial changes in their lives. They will come, because they now see that Jesus – and the salvation he offers – is the ultimate treasure.

Yet the evidence shows us that the disciples were still at least partly blind to the call of Jesus to deny themselves. After he explained about his mission again in Mark 9:30-32, we discover in 9:33-34 that the disciples responded by arguing among themselves about which of them was the greatest. Then, in spite of Jesus' clear correction in 9:35-37 and again in 10:13-14, we find James and John wanting to share glory with Jesus in 10:35-37.

They were still struggling to see the implications of the call of Jesus on their lives. Peter famously denied knowing Jesus, rather than denying himself, for fear of the implications of being his disciple.

Yet the Lord Jesus graciously and patiently worked with them during his years of public ministry, before and after his death and resurrection. The journey of the disciples to properly seeing who Jesus is, why he came and what it means to follow him is the journey that many course members are on. This makes Mark's Gospel a great book for evangelism.

Understanding the identity, mission and call of Jesus is the core of Mark's message, and the basis of salvation. Talking to course members about these three great themes in Mark, and asking them who they think Jesus is, why he came and what it means to follow him, is a great way to work out where they are spiritually, and how we can help them move forward.

Running the sessions

PREPARING BEFORE THE GROUP ARRIVES

Arrive in plenty of time so that you can pray with the other leaders. Pray for individual group members, asking God to open their blind eyes and to help them understand who Jesus is, why he came and what it means to follow him.

Use the "big idea" printed in this Leader's Guide at the start of each session to pray that people will understand and respond to the specific teaching for that session. Pray too for one another.

Everyone on the course – leaders and group members – will need a Mark's Gospel or Bible. For the sake of clarity, it is important that everyone uses the same version. (The version used throughout the course material is the 1984 edition of the New International Version (NIV). If you are using the 2011 NIV, you will find that there are some changes in parts of the text. If these changes affect any of the discussion questions, you will find a note explaining the changes at the relevant point in this Leader's Guide.)

Make sure you have enough copies of the group member's Handbook so that everyone can have their own copy – and some spares if people take their copies home between sessions.

There is a "leader's checklist" in this Leader's Guide at the start of each session. This will help you make sure you have everything you need.

PREPARING THE ROOM

Think about the type of people coming and make them feel as relaxed as possible. Make sure they know where the toilet is. Think about...

■ **Seating.** Are there any special seating needs for the guests (eg: bad backs, older people who don't want to be seated too low)? People with hearing problems might need to be nearer the leader. If you are using the DVD, everyone needs to see the screen comfortably. Try not to have the group leader sitting with their back to a window since this can make it hard for others to see his/her face. Some groups might enjoy a more "seminar-style" format where people sit around a table to discuss. This makes it easier to juggle Bibles/Mark's Gospels and Handbooks.

- **Lighting.** Check that it is adequate so that people can easily see what they are reading.

- **Room temperature.** Make sure it is comfortable before people arrive.

- **Pets.** Put them in another room until you know if all the guests are comfortable with them.

You might like to put on some fairly neutral background music – popular jazz is often a good option. Be careful of pushing your particular eccentric tastes in music. But remember, this is to be in the background to set the atmosphere – not too loud or it will make chatting together difficult. Turn the music off when you get started.

If you are preparing a meal, check if people have any dietary requirements. Avoid pork and beef with people from a Muslim, Jewish or Hindu background. If you are not sharing a meal together, have a pot of coffee/tea ready, a jug of fruit juice and some water.

Think of some subjects to talk about beforehand so that, as you are drinking and waiting for others to arrive, there won't be embarrassing silences. You may not need them, but be prepared.

WELCOMING GROUP MEMBERS

- **Remember their names.** This makes people feel valued and respected. Use name badges if it makes this easier.

- **Take the lead in introducing people to each other.** Always introduce new guests. If you know some background that is relevant, then use that as well. "Let me introduce you to Fred. He works in the building trade too." "Li is from South Korea and is studying mathematics." "Sarah has two boys at Bean Road School as well."

- **Make sure there is time for people to relax and talk to each other** before you begin. This greatly helps the discussion later.

Sit where you can see everyone. That way, you can make eye contact with people, and it also ensures that they can see you too. It's not a good idea for leaders to sit next to one another, as this can look intimidating. Why not save your seat before others arrive, with your Bible or jacket?

LEADING THE BIBLE STUDY

After everyone has arrived and you've had time to relax and chat together over a meal or coffee, begin the Bible-study time. As leader, your responsibility is more than just asking the Bible-study questions. You should try to maintain a relaxed atmosphere and involve everyone in the discussion if possible. Don't forget how important the tone of your voice and your body language can be as you lead the discussion.

Each study follows the same pattern:

- **Discuss any questions.** At the start of the study, if group members have been reading Mark at home, ask if they have any questions about what they read. Discuss as necessary. Since not everyone will have read Mark at home, be careful not to make anyone feel uncomfortable. If nobody has anything they'd like to discuss, move on.

- **Recap.** Briefly summarise what has been covered in previous sessions. There is a box in the group member's Handbook, at the start of each session, labelled "The story so far". This will help you give a short summary.

- **Opening discussion question(s).** These questions are designed to open up discussion. Don't spend too long over them. The aim is just to get people talking.

- **Read aloud from Mark.** Asking a group member to do this may make them feel uncomfortable, so you or a co-leader should read the passage. The exception is with language learners or international students who may have come because they want to practise their English and are therefore keen to read aloud. Once the passage has been read out, let the group read it again silently. If anyone has English as a second language, encourage them to read the passage in their own language as well.

- **Bible words.** These word lists pick out difficult words from the passage in Mark and define them in simple English. It is a good idea to make sure that everyone understands these words before starting the Bible Study questions. You will know your group. If they need you to go through the words one at a time, do it, but if not, keep going. If you have some members who are not struggling with English and some who are, ask the confident ones to help those who are struggling.

- **Questions on Mark.** The passage is usually split into smaller sections to make the study easier, or there may be more than one passage during the study. It is

25

worth reading each section again before you discuss it. This helps in terms of language, and encourages people to look to Scripture for the answers.

It is important to listen carefully to the answers given and to reply graciously. Your group need to know that they are valued and that their opinions are important to you. If appropriate for your group, encourage them to write down the answers in the space provided in their Handbook. Notes on the answers are provided for you in the second section of this Leader's Guide, but it's a good idea to write your own notes into a handbook, so that you can work from the same book as your group.

SUMMARIES OF WHAT HAS BEEN LEARNED

At the end of each study, and sometimes during it, there is a short summary of what has been learned. Some of these summaries also have a simple picture alongside them. A leader should read each summary aloud as you come to it.

FINISHING

- **DVD.** At the end of the Bible Study, you could show the *Christianity Explored* DVD as a summary of what you have been discussing. But be aware that the DVD may introduce passages or concepts that are not covered in the Bible study so it is important that you watch it beforehand. You will then be able to judge whether it will or will not be helpful for your group and situation.

- **Limit the study time to between 1 and 1 ¹/₂ hours.** You should be able to complete the study in that time, but if you are behind schedule, don't rush through the questions. Instead, complete as many as you can and consider finishing the study at the start of your next meeting.

- **Always finish at the promised time.** Good timekeeping develops trust in the group, and people will be more likely to return next week. However, let group members know that they are welcome to stay and talk further if they like.

Time spent talking with people after the study officially ends gives you a great opportunity to explore where individuals are in their understanding of the gospel message. Try to help them understand things they are struggling with. Encourage them by talking about your own conversion and Christian life if appropriate. Many people ignore the Christian faith because they feel it is not relevant to their own experience of real life, so use this time to apply Christian thinking to their situation. Help them to see the need for a personal response to Jesus Christ, but do not pressurize them.

READING MARK AT HOME

It may be appropriate to ask group members to read part of Mark's Gospel before the next session. Pages 37-39 of the Handbook will help them to do this. Each section of Mark is divided into five passages. If you are meeting weekly, you may like to suggest that they read one passage a day rather than try and read the whole section at one time. Explain that there will be time to discuss briefly what they have read next week.

Reading through the whole of Mark's Gospel will be hugely helpful, but for some individuals or groups, this may feel too difficult or time consuming. They may even feel they can't come back to the next session if they haven't done their "homework". Reassure them that coming to the group is more important than managing to read Mark at home. It's also fine not to mention the home reading at all. This section of the material has been put at the back of the Handbook for this reason, so that people will not feel they "ought" to be doing it after each session.

What to do if...

... THERE'S SILENCE

If a question is met with silence, don't be too quick to speak. Allow people time to think. They might be considering how to phrase their answer. Remember that in some cultures it is considered rude to speak immediately after the previous person; therefore a short silence (even up to 30 seconds) is the polite norm.

If you sense that someone knows the answer but is shy about giving it, ask them by name. Often they will be happy to be asked.

It may help to divide people into groups of two or three to work through questions and then have them feed their answers back to the whole group.

... ONE PERSON ANSWERS ALL THE QUESTIONS

- Thank them for their answer, then ask: "What do other people think?"

- Direct a few questions at the other group members by name. (But if it seems awkward, open up the question to the rest of the group.)

- Sit beside the talkative person the following week. That will make it harder for them to catch your eye and answer the questions.

- If the issue continues, talk to the person after the study and ask them to give others time to answer, eg: "Thank you so much for all you're contributing. I wonder if you can help me with the quieter people in the group..."

... SOMEONE GIVES THE WRONG ANSWER

- **Do not immediately correct them.** Give the person the opportunity to correct themselves. Ask them, for example: "What does verse 4 tell us about that?" If they are still unable to answer correctly, give others the chance, eg: "Does anyone disagree or want to add anything?".

- **Graciously correct.** If necessary, don't be afraid graciously to correct a wrong answer that may mislead others. Say something like: "Thank you, that's an interesting point, but I'm not sure that's what's going on here".

■ **Ask further questions.** Eg: "What do you mean by that?" or "Where does it say that?" or "What does everyone else think?" If no one can answer, give the correct answer, showing from the Bible passage why it is right.

... SOMEONE ASKS A QUESTION YOU CANNOT ANSWER

■ **Lead honestly.** You won't be able to answer every question. Some questions can be easily addressed, but others will be difficult. If you don't know the answer, say so – but tell them that you'll try to find out for the next time. (There are lists of common questions and answers starting on page 125.)

■ **Lend a book.** It may be best to give someone a suitable book to help them. See www.ceministries.org for suggestions.

... PEOPLE DON'T COME BACK

Don't pursue them. In Mark 4, Jesus taught us to expect negative as well as positive responses to the gospel message. However, if you've already established a good relationship with that person, contact him or her once to say you missed them and that it would be great to see them next week, but don't put pressure on them.

... GROUP MEMBERS MISS A WEEK OR MORE

Welcome them back and during the meal/coffee time try and summarize what they have missed. If appropriate, encourage them to make time later to read the passages in Mark they've missed and to go through the questions in the Handbook. Let them know they can come back to you with anything they do not understand.

If someone misses most of the course, encourage them to do it again. This could be with another group, or you may be able to do the material with them one to one.

... THEY RAISE A PASTORAL ISSUE YOU CAN'T DEAL WITH

It is best not to try and deal with situations if you feel you are out of your depth. Encourage the person to go with you to see your pastor or a Christian counsellor.

Offer to pray with them about the issue.

Do not break their confidence without asking their permission first. However, in extreme circumstances you may need to do so even if they refuse permission.

Working with English speakers

The *Christianity Explored Universal Edition* has been developed for use with a wide range of people. The questions and explanations have been written to be simple, but not shallow. We have not "dumbed down" the content, even if we have tried to express it in clear language. So we hope that this resource will find wide use with people who are native English speakers. But we hope that it will also prove useful to those with limited literary skills, who might not be used to reading much.

A few things to bear in mind are:

ATMOSPHERE

Some people are easily intimidated by the idea of studying, for practical and/or cultural reasons, so it will be important to avoid a classroom atmosphere.

- Think about how you arrange your venue – comfortable and informal rather than functional and formal.

- Be warm and friendly, and use humour. Reassure people that there are no exams or marks, and no passing or failing involved in the course.

- Be clear in your own mind about the goal of *Christianity Explored* but flexible about how that goal is achieved (eg: not everyone needs to write down answers in their booklets).

- Try to avoid using educational terms (see table below).

Avoid	Use
study	look at
a study, a Bible study	a session
course	Christianity Explored
students	group members, guests, people
teacher	group leader
homework	preparing for next session

Note: *If your group is made up of internationals who are learning English, they will be comfortable with the idea of a course of study and may be attracted to your group for this reason. See page 33 for more about working with internationals.*

OPPORTUNITIES TO PREPARE

Some people may be unwilling to answer any questions in the session, however much you rephrase things or give them ideas. This may be a lack of confidence, rather than lack of understanding. They may prefer to go through the questions and, if they wish, write down some answers before coming to the session.

Make this optional for those who will find it beneficial. Some will not bother, some will take the opportunity just to read through the Bible passage and questions, while some will try to complete the whole session. Make sure they understand that no one is going to "mark" their answers.

READING AND WRITING

If your group have limited literacy skills, any reading aloud should be done by a leader. Never expect the people in your group do this. It would be good to read aloud both the Bible passage and the questions in the Handbook.

Some people may be intimidated by having to handle a whole Bible packed with small type. We have prepared sheets of the individual NIV passages in Mark in a reader-friendly format that you can download and print out (visit www.ceministries.org). Encourage your group to underline, circle or highlight key words and phrases, so that they can more easily read and understand the passage. If the group struggles with NIV, we suggest you try either NIrV or NCV.

Any writing should also be optional. People may struggle with writing and may prefer to do any out of sight of the group. Provide pens and pencils in a central, easily accessible place, rather than allocating one to each person, so that people don't feel they are expected to write something.

BREAKS

Providing breaks will be more important for some groups than others. Be aware that some people may find the session quite intensive and tiring, especially if they have no experience of church or of meeting with Christians. Allow a few moments for people to go outside to smoke a cigarette, use the toilets or just stretch their legs and get some fresh air.

Cross-cultural evangelism

There may be people from a number of different cultures in your group, so it is important to be aware of some specific issues.

Crucially, you will need to keep in mind at all times that those in your group live between two cultures, two sets of values, two ways of living. You will therefore have to address the topics raised during *Christianity Explored Universal* in both contexts.

As well as helping them understand the gospel, this is important because, without appropriate teaching and support, new Christians will struggle to maintain their faith and share it with others when they go home. Experience has shown that if they are not expecting and not equipped to deal with their return home, then a large proportion will end up not living the Christian life at all, and may not even be claiming to be Christians any more. Obviously, things will differ for each individual case but there are some basic principles that you can apply as you lead your group.

THE IMPORTANCE OF RELATIONSHIPS

In many cultures around the world, an individual's identity is rooted in a group (see page 36 for more on this). This group may be the family, peer group, or work colleagues. Personal opinions are often considered less important than the group's opinion.

Obviously this can have negative implications for Bible-study groups. People may be hesitant to share their own questions or their own response to the gospel message. So it's important to encourage an atmosphere that will help to overcome these reservations.

- Holding the Bible studies in someone's house is better than meeting in a coffee shop or public space.

- Sharing a meal together before the Bible study will help people relax.

- Be sensitive to the behaviour of those from other cultures. The apostle Paul adapted his behaviour in order to win as many as possible from different backgrounds: "I have become all things to all men so that by all possible means I might save some. I do all this for the sake of the gospel, that I may share in its blessings"

(1 Corinthians 9:22-23). This means watching, learning and following cultural cues. It might include addressing group members in a particular way; being careful not to point at people; if you share a meal, not eating with your left hand, and so on. With a group made up of many cultures, however, it is impossible to be aware of, or to adapt your behaviour to, every culture within the group. Don't spend time worrying about making cultural blunders. People will forgive you if they can see that you genuinely care about them.

• Group outings outside of your weekly meetings will help relationships to grow – for example, playing a sport or going to an appropriate film.

• Don't lose touch afterwards. After the course has finished, whether or not group members have become Christians, try to stay in contact.

GROUP DISCUSSIONS

The idea of "group discussions" might be strange to some people. In many Asian cultures, for example, the "teacher" is expected to give information, while the "student" passively absorbs.

In some cultures it is considered a virtue to remain silent, rather than bother the teacher or hold up the group.

• Explain that the group will learn together from the Bible, and that it is a discussion, not a lecture.

• Tell the group that it is important for them to share their ideas, and that you are not expecting them to always have the correct answer.

• Make it clear to group members that they are free to ask questions whenever they want, and that no question is too simple or difficult.

• If you find the group dynamic still does not work, it may be that people are only used to group discussion in a single-sex environment. You may want to consider splitting them into single-sex groups.

LANGUAGE BARRIERS

If some or all of your group are struggling to speak English, they may feel embarrassed and therefore be reluctant to contribute to the discussion.

Sometimes, when people come from the same country, they may fear "losing face" or being embarrassed in front of their friends if they don't understand.

In addition, studying the Bible will probably introduce new words to the group.

However, for many, the attraction of studying Mark's Gospel in English will outweigh the language struggles they may experience.

The leader's notes for each session suggest that, after reading the passage in English, group members read it again in their own language. This will not only help them to understand the passage, but also to get used to explaining the gospel message and concepts they have learned in their own language. This will help them when they return home. and avoid others seeing their beliefs as merely a "western message".

Bible translations in most languages are available on the internet (visit www.bible-gateway.com) and can be used side by side with an English translation. Bilingual Bibles are also available in some languages.

- As you prepare the Bible study at home, anticipate which words might be new to people. Be prepared to explain them simply and clearly. You will also find a list of Bible words (and other words that may not be familiar to internationals) alongside each session in the group member's Handbook. These word lists are also included within each session in this Leader's Guide.

- After a passage is read, you may want to ask your group: "Are there any words you do not understand?" Initially group members might be shy to admit this, so you may simply choose to go through some or all of the words in the Bible words list in their Handbooks.

- Be creative in your presentation. Use pictures, diagrams and illustrations to explain difficult words or concepts.

- Bear in mind that words and phrases familiar to Christians (for example, "pagan", "washed in the blood", "house group", "the Lord" and so on) may seem strange to those from other cultures.

EXPLAINING THE GOSPEL TO THOSE OF OTHER FAITHS

The Bible teaches that salvation is only possible through faith in Jesus Christ: "I am the way and the truth and the life. No-one comes to the Father except through me" (John 14:6); "Salvation is found in no-one else, for there is no other name under heaven given to men by which we must be saved" (Acts 4:12). While always being respectful towards people of other religions, we must hold firmly to the Bible's teaching on the uniqueness of Christ.

- In Romans 10:17 the apostle Paul explains that: "Faith comes from hearing the message, and the message is heard through the word of Christ". That means that you do not need a thorough understanding of Islam or the Qur'an before you can share the gospel with a Muslim. Nor do you need to be familiar with folk religion before sharing the gospel with someone who practises it. Although it may be considerate to have some background knowledge of other religions, it is the clear presentation of the gospel message that leads to faith.

- Religions may share words such as "God", "sin", "eternal life" and so on – but the meanings of these words are often very different. For example, to a Muslim, God is impersonal and distant. He does not love people or desire a relationship with them. To a Buddhist, the prospect of eternal life is something to be avoided, not celebrated. To a Hindu, Jesus Christ can be one among many gods, rather than the unique revelation of the only God. When appropriate, explain what the Bible means by these terms.

WHERE DOES OUR IDENTITY COME FROM?

Our culture affects our identity from the core of our being to our external actions. Our understanding of who we are is deeply affected by the culture in which we grew up. Much of western society is founded on the core idea/value of individualism, ie: from childhood people are taught the principle "I am because I am". The most important thing is to "be yourself". Being independent is seen as a commendable quality. Much of the western education system is aimed at teaching children to become independent. They are taught that their opinion matters; therefore, in a discussion group everyone's contribution is valuable and should be expressed. This is why most westerners do not have a problem disagreeing with their teacher.

In many cultures around the world, people's core understanding of who they are is based on a different premise: "I am because we are" is the core value/idea. Therefore, the primary commitment in people's morals is to the group that they belong to (family, ethnic group etc). To look after your group is the most important thing.

When people become Christians, it is not simply their external actions that need to be transformed; it is their whole understanding of their identity. If the gospel only affects the externals, then we have a problem. Christianity is not an extra layer to be added to our identity – but needs to be at the core of our identity.

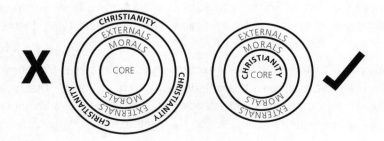

If people live for any period of time outside their own culture, they begin to take on some of the externals of their host culture or even adopt some of the morals. For example, an international student in the UK may become more individualistic. They might learn to challenge their lecturers when they think they are wrong. But when they return home, they quickly discover that the way they think and act causes friction with people back home. So, in time, people usually decide to adapt back to the cultural norm.

So, if an international student becomes a Christian while studying in the UK, we need to ask: will they see their faith as something that is bound to their British culture, something that can be discarded when the going gets tough? Or have they been helped to grapple with how the gospel affects every area of their life right to their core understanding of who they are? Is their new identity in *Christ* or is it in their *culture*? If their faith has not penetrated to the core, then, when the going gets tough, it will be discarded along with the elements of British culture that have caused them so much trouble as they adapt to life back home.

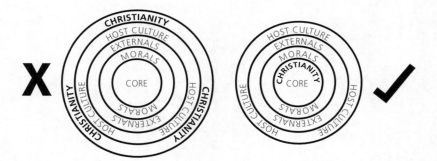

If we disciple people effectively, then Christianity will not be an added-on external layer but an integral part of their identity. Their identity has to be in Christ if they are to persevere in the midst of the difficult transition back to their home country. This means that we must attempt to narrow the perceived gap between their understanding of what it means to be a Christian in the two cultures they live between.

You want the group to understand what it means to live for Christ and to find their identity securely in him.

One resource that can help you to disciple new Christians, and prepare them for their return home, is *Discipleship Explored Universal* (see www.ceministries.org/de). This course takes people through the book of Philippians and is an ideal follow up to *Christianity Explored Universal*. It includes help and advice for discipling internationals and preparing them for their return to their own country. It also includes an International Student Edition of the group member's Study Guide.

38

After the course

Christianity Explored is not an eight-session conveyor belt that either ships unbelievers into the Christian faith – or tips them off into the street outside. It is therefore vital to have a coherent follow-up strategy in place for all guests.

GIVE OUT FEEDBACK FORMS

Feedback forms, given out during the last session of the course, are a great way to challenge course members to think about where they currently are with Christ, and to help leaders plan a way forward once the course is ended.

You can find a sample feedback form on page 40. An editable version of this form can be downloaded from **www.ceministries.org**

STAY IN TOUCH

Having spent eight sessions with your group considering profound and personal issues, you will know them well – and they will know you well.

Under these circumstances, it would clearly be wrong to "drop" group members once the course comes to an end. Whatever their response has been, God has not given up on them, and neither should you.

Furthermore, if the friends who invited these people along see leaders maintaining a genuine interest in the guests, they will feel more confident about bringing others along in future.

Plan to stay in touch with all the members of your group, and arrange it with your co-leaders so that each group member has at least one Christian who remains in touch with him or her.

Feedback Form

You don't have to answer all the questions if you don't want to, but please be as honest as you can.

Your details (optional):

Name _____ Date _____

Address _____

Telephone _____ Email _____

1. Before you began *Christianity Explored*, how would you have described yourself?

☐ I didn't believe in God

☐ I wasn't sure if God existed or not

☐ I believed in God but not in Jesus Christ

☐ A Christian (that is, personally committed to Jesus Christ)

☐ Something else _____

2. How would you describe yourself now in relation to Jesus Christ?

☐ I understand who Jesus is, why he came and what it means to follow him. I have put my trust in him.

☐ I am interested in learning more but, as yet, I have not put my trust in Jesus.

☐ Other _____

3. If you have not yet put your trust in Jesus, what is stopping you?

4. Do you know for certain that you have eternal life?

☐ Yes ☐ No

5. Suppose you were to die tonight and God asked: "Why should I let you into heaven?" What would you say?

6. What would you like to do now?

☐ I would like to join *Discipleship Explored* (a course that will help me to continue in the Christian life).

☐ I would like to come to *Christianity Explored* again.

☐ I would like a copy of the *Christianity Explored* book to remind me of what I've learned.

☐ I do not wish to do anything further at this stage.

☐ I would like to join a church.

☐ I am happy at the church I go to, which is _____

7. Would you like to make any comments about the course, either positive or negative?

ARRANGE FOLLOW-UP FOR NEW BELIEVERS

If anyone in your group has made a commitment to Christ, it's vital to help them lay firm foundations so that they will be able to persevere.

Discipleship Explored Universal, based on the book of Philippians, is one way of doing this. The *Discipleship Explored Universal* course has a similar format to *Christianity Explored Universal* and lasts for eight sessions. You can find out more about *Discipleship Explored Universal* at **www.ceministries.org**

You should also invite new believers to start coming along to church with you if they're not already regularly attending. It is often a difficult task to get people into the habit of meeting together regularly on a Sunday, but the concept of a Christian who doesn't belong to a church is foreign to the New Testament, so help them to take this seriously (Hebrews 10:25). Introduce them to other Christians and help them to become integrated within the church by joining a Bible-study group and finding an area of service within which they can participate.

ARRANGE FOLLOW-UP FOR THOSE WHO HAVEN'T YET MADE A COMMITMENT

Ask whether they are interested in exploring Christianity further. If they are, one option is to invite them to come back and go through *Christianity Explored Universal* again – some people have gone through the course three or more times before they felt ready to make a commitment. Remember that they will be re-reading Mark's Gospel each time, which will work on their hearts whenever it is opened.

RECOMMEND OR GIVE AWAY BOOKS

If appropriate for your group member, reading a good Christian book at the right time can be very influential. Think carefully about the books you've read and see if any of them would suit particular people. If you're not an avid reader, ask around for advice about books suitable for people in different situations.[1]

Alternatively, you could encourage people to spend some time looking at the testimonies and videos on the *Christianity Explored* website. There is also an animated gospel summary. See **www.christianityexplored.org**

---

1   Two paperbacks accompany the *Christianity Explored* course: "One life. What's it all about?" and "If you could ask God one question...". You could also look at the "Go Deeper" sections in the Tough Questions area of the *Christianity Explored* website (choose a question from www.christianityexplored.org/tough-questions, and then click on the "Go Deeper" bar).

READ THE BIBLE WITH A GROUP MEMBER

You might suggest getting together with an individual on a regular basis to read through a book of the Bible. This can be totally informal; just two friends with an open Bible finding out what God's word has to say to them.

Questions to guide your study could be:

What does the passage mean?

■ Are there any difficult words or ideas that need special attention?

What does the passage mean in context?

■ What comes before/after the passage?

■ Why is the passage placed where it is?

■ Is it addressed to a specific individual or group of people? Why?

What does the passage mean for us?

■ What have we learned about ourselves?

■ About God?

■ How do we apply the passage to our lives?

PRAY

A supremely Christ-like way of caring for people is to pray for them. Even after the course has ended, it is important to pray for all the members of the group.

For new believers, pray for growth, fruitfulness and joy.

For those who have not yet made a commitment, pray that the Lord will have mercy on them and send his Holy Spirit to open their blind eyes.

Pray for yourself, for patience and wisdom as you wait for God's word to do its work.

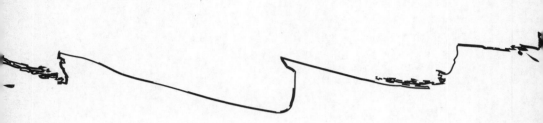

Study Guide

Two *Christianity Explored* websites to help you:

www.christianityexplored.org
This website is for non-Christians, whether or not they are on a course. It features a visual gospel outline based on the Gospel of Mark, answers to common questions, and testimonies from a wide variety of people, as well as information about the *Christianity Explored* course. You can find more details at the back of this book, on page 143.

www.ceministries.org
For leaders looking for information, downloads and resources.

Introduction

This Study Guide section contains notes on the eight Bible studies to help you lead *Christianity Explored Universal*. It includes all the material in the group members' Handbook. However it also contains specific instructions for leaders, additional notes and the answers to each question.

- Don't worry if you don't have time to go through all of the questions with your group – the most important thing is to listen to the group members and answer their questions.

- Try to avoid using "jargon" that might alienate group members. Bear in mind that words and phrases familiar to Christians (for example, "pagan," "washed in the blood," "house group," "the Lord" and so on) may seem strange to those outside Christian circles.

- If group members miss a week, take time to summarize briefly what was taught the week before. There are short summaries at the start of each session in the Handbook to help you do this.

- Some guests may believe that the Bible is not reliable as a source of history. If this issue arises during a group discussion, there is a section on the reliability of Mark's Gospel on page 139 of this Leader's Guide.

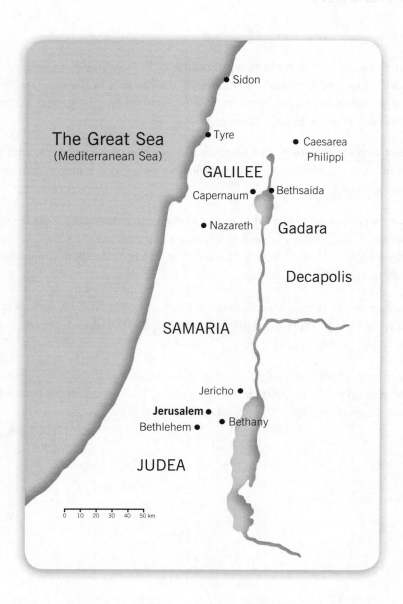

The Great Sea
(Mediterranean Sea)

Sidon

Tyre

Caesarea
Philippi

GALILEE

Capernaum

Bethsaida

Nazareth

Gadara

Decapolis

SAMARIA

Jericho

Jerusalem

Bethlehem

Bethany

JUDEA

0 10 20 30 40 50 km

Note: This map is printed on page 4 of the group members' Handbook. You may find it helpful to refer to it occasionally when reading about events that happen in particular places. You could perhaps say: "Mark tells us about the amazing things Jesus did and said. He also tells us where Jesus was at the time. We will use the map to help us follow the story as Jesus travels around the country of Israel."

What is Christianity?

THE BIG IDEA

Christianity is the good news about Jesus Christ.

📧 *Welcome the group members to Christianity Explored and introduce yourself. Make sure everyone has been introduced to each other. Try to remember names ready for next time.*

📧 *Give a brief introduction. The wording below is intended only as a general guide – please adapt it to your particular situation (see pages 31 and 33).*

As we begin, I want you to know that:

🔲 You won't be asked to read aloud, pray, sing or do anything that makes you feel uncomfortable.

🔲 We aren't going to take your phone number and pester you. If you decide not to come back, we are still delighted you made time to come today.

🔲 You can ask any question you want, or if you prefer, feel free just to sit and listen.

📧 *Give each person a Mark's Gospel, Bible or printout of the Bible passages (in their own language if needed) and a copy of the Christianity Explored Universal Handbook.*

📧 *Ask the group to turn to "Before we begin" on page 4 of the Handbook. Read it out to your group and point out the map (see opposite). You may want to explain that Mark didn't divide his book into chapters (the large numbers) and verses (the small numbers). These were added later to help us find our way around.*

📧 *Ask the group to turn to Session 1 on page 5 of the Handbook.*

Leader's checklist

Have you...

🔲 Made it clear to people the time and place where you will meet?

🔲 Prepared food and drinks?

🔲 Enough Gospels, Bibles or sheets with the Bible passages on them (see page 12)?

🔲 Christianity Explored Universal Handbooks for each person?

🔲 Name labels, if appropriate?

🔲 Thought through your answers to each of the questions?

🔲 Prayed for each group member and yourself as the leader?

🔲 The optional Christianity Explored DVD ready to play?

OPENING DISCUSSION QUESTIONS

Ask your group the following questions. The first one is not in the Handbook.

What's your name and why have you come to *Christianity Explored*?

This question is designed to help the group members get to know each other, and to help you begin to understand why they have come on the course.

If you could ask God one question, and you knew it would be answered, what would it be?

Ask your group to share their answers if they're happy to do so. Note down what they are so that you can deal with them at some point during the eight sessions. Don't try to answer all the questions now, but do listen carefully to every question and assure group members that there will be an opportunity to return to them during *Christianity Explored*. (Some questions will be answered by the Bible studies and some – like questions about suffering – are best dealt with after the sessions about sin or the cross.) *See page 133 for guidance on common questions.*

You may also like to ask your group:

Think about the god you are asking that question to. What do you think that god is like?

This will help you to get a feel for people's current views of God. You may want to refer back to some of these views later on in the course, as the character of God becomes clear through his Son, Jesus.

What do many people think Christianity is about?
- [ ] **Christianity is about being a good person**
- [ ] **Christianity is about going to church**
- [ ] **Christianity is a western religion**
- [ ] **Christianity is about following the teachings of Jesus Christ**
- [ ] **Christianity is** _____

This question asks what most people think Christianity is about. Don't make your group members feel uncomfortable by asking what they think personally.

Explain that you will be looking at the Gospel of Mark, part of the Bible, to see what Mark says Christianity is about. This is explained at the bottom of page 5 of the Handbook which says:

> **Christianity Explored takes us through the Gospel of Mark so that we can discover the real answer to the question: "What is Christianity?"**

You may want to read aloud the section "Who was Mark?" from page 5 of the Handbook. It says this:

> **Mark was a friend and companion of Peter, who was one of Jesus' closest friends. Peter was an "apostle", someone chosen to tell other people about the life, death and resurrection (rising from death) of Jesus.**
>
> **Peter wrote two of the letters in the Bible (known as 1 and 2 Peter). In his second letter he said: "I will make every effort to see that after my departure (death) you will always remember these things" (2 Peter 1:15). He meant the things he saw and knew about Jesus. He passed them on to others like Mark.**
>
> **Peter died about 30 years after Jesus died. The evidence tells us that Mark wrote his book around then. Mark's Gospel is one of four books in the Bible telling the life story of Jesus. The others were written by Matthew, Luke and John.**

BIBLE DISCUSSION

▨ *Ask the group members to turn to Mark 1:1 in their Gospels, Bibles or printed sheets.*

👁 **Read aloud Mark 1:1**

▨ *Note: Christianity Explored is based on the 1984 version of the New International Version (NIV). If you are using the 2011 revised NIV, you will find that "Jesus Christ" in Mark 1:1 has been changed to "Jesus the Messiah". The change from "Christ" to "Messiah" does not change the meaning of the verse, since both words mean the same. They are titles for the King who God promised to send into the world. "Christ" is from the Greek word; "Messiah" comes from the Hebrew.*

▨ *If your group members have English as a second language, encourage them to read the verse a second time in their own language. This will help them to understand the passage better. It will also help them if and when they return home – see page 33.*

There is a list of Bible words from this week's passages (NIV) on pages 6-7 of the group member's Handbook. Depending on your group, it may be appropriate to go through some or all of these words at this point. The word list for this study is also shown below.

Bible words	
Mark 1:1 **v1 gospel.** Good news. **v1 Christ/Messiah.** God's only chosen King, who God promised to send into the world.	**v9 Galilee.** The northern area of the country of Israel. See map on page 4 (*of the Handbook*). **v9 baptized.** John baptized people in the Jordan river by dipping them under the water. Baptism is a symbol or picture of turning away from sin and being washed clean on the inside.
Mark 1:9-11 **v9 Nazareth.** A town in the north of the country of Israel. Jesus grew up in Nazareth. See map on page 4 (*of the Handbook*).	**v10 Spirit.** The Holy Spirit. The Bible teaches that there is one God in three persons: God the Father, God the Son (that's Jesus) and God the Holy Spirit.

Re-read Mark 1:1

1. What do we learn about Christianity from this verse?

Christianity is about Jesus Christ. You may want to explain that "Christ" isn't Jesus' surname. It is a title that means "God's only chosen King".

The word "gospel" means "good news", so Christianity is good news about Jesus Christ.

2. Some people criticise Christianity. They say:

   "It is a list of rules."

   "It is about going to church and pretending to be a good person."

   "It is boring."

   How does Mark answer these criticisms in Mark 1:1?

Christianity is none of these things. It is good news about a person, Jesus Christ.

This is the "big Idea" for this session (see page 49) so make sure your group members have grasped it. For this reason the rest of the course will be exploring what Mark tells us about Jesus.

👁 **Read aloud Mark 1:9-11**

💬 *If your group members have English as a second language, encourage them to read the passage a second time in their own language.*

💬 *Depending on your group, it may be appropriate to go through some or all of the Bible words listed on page 7 of the Handbook at this point. The word list for this study is also shown opposite.*

👁 **Re-read Mark 1:9-11**

Jesus was baptized by John in the Jordan river. As Jesus came up out of the water, God the Holy Spirit came down on him in the form of a dove, and God the Father spoke.

3. What did God the Father say about Jesus?

God said three things about Jesus:

1) Jesus is his Son

2) He loves Jesus

3) He is very pleased with Jesus.

Mark has already told us that Jesus is the Christ, God's only chosen King. The important thing we learn here is that Jesus is also the Son of God. We will find out more about both of these in the next session, which looks at who Jesus is.

Note: For Muslim group members, Jesus being the Son of God is a huge barrier and massive question. You will need to discuss this further in session 2.

4. Is there anything that surprises, interests or puzzles you about Jesus?

The answers to this question will help you to get a feel for the members of your group and their current thoughts about Jesus. Don't feel that you need to comment on everything they say – there will be plenty of time during the course to address any wrong ideas. However, if you know that something will be looked at in a future session, do let the group members know that you will be discussing it at that point. This will encourage them to keep coming.

▣ *Read the summary printed on page 7 of the Handbook. It says:*

Christianity is the good news (the "gospel") about Jesus Christ.

Mark tells us that Jesus is God's chosen King, known as the Christ or Messiah. Mark also shows that Jesus is the Son of God.

CHAPTER 1 - Good News
18 MINS

▣ *If you feel it is appropriate for your group, you may like to show episode 1 of the* Christianity Explored *DVD at this point. The DVD can be used as a summary or a refresher for the main teaching point of this session. However, it also includes Bible passages and concepts that have not been covered in this Bible study, so please watch it in advance to judge whether or not your group members would find it helpful.*

▣ *If it's appropriate for your group, ask them to read Mark 1:1 – 3:12 before the next session. There's space at the back of the group member's Handbook, on page 37, for them to write down any questions they have. Group members will benefit from reading through Mark's Gospel while doing* Christianity Explored *– but this may be too much for some to attempt. It's more important that they feel able to come back to the group next time, rather than worrying that they've been unable to do their "homework".*

▣ *Thank your group members for coming and encourage them to come back next time. Tell them:* We've seen that Mark says that Christianity is all about one man, Jesus. Next time we'll find out about some of the things that Jesus did and said, and why Mark says that Jesus is "good news".

AFTERWARDS

▣ Did you manage to keep the focus on the big idea of this session?

▣ Write down the questions that people have come up with, so that you can be sure to look at them in the coming sessions. It may be helpful at this point to prepare a plan of which question you deal with each session.

▣ Think about the people who came. Make a list so that you can pray for them.

▣ Are there any practical arrangements you need to do differently next time? (Eg: did you have enough Bibles/Gospels/printed sheets?)

Who is Jesus?

2

THE BIG IDEA

Jesus has the power and authority of God, including the authority to forgive sin. He is the Son of God.

▸ Ask everyone to turn to Session 2 on page 9 of the *Christianity Explored Universal Handbook*.

▸ If you suggested that your group read Mark 1:1 – 3:6 at home, ask if they have any questions about what they read – but be careful to leave enough time for the study. The appendix on page 125 lists common questions from Mark along with suggestions for answering them.

▸ Read the summary of Session 1, called "The story so far", on page 9 of the Handbook. It says:

• **Christianity is about Jesus Christ.**

• **It is the good news (the "gospel") about Jesus.**

• **When Jesus was baptized by John, God's voice was heard. God called Jesus his Son.**

▸ Explain that in this session we will find out more about Jesus by looking at the evidence in Mark's Gospel. Mark gives us information so that we can build up an accurate, historical picture of who Jesus was.

Leader's checklist

Have you...

☐ Reminded group members where and when you will meet (eg: by email or text message)?

☐ Prepared food and drinks?

☐ Enough Gospels, Bibles or printed-out sheets with the Bible passages on them (and copies in the group member's first language if appropriate – see page 12)?

☐ Handbooks for each person, plus spares if needed?

☐ Thought through your answers to each of the questions?

☐ Prayed for each group member and yourself as the leader?

☐ The optional Christianity Explored DVD ready to play?

OPENING DISCUSSION QUESTION

🗨 *Ask your group the following question.*

Who do your friends or family think Jesus is?

☐ **A good teacher**

☐ **A prophet**

☐ **A political leader**

☐ **The Son of God** ✓

☐ **Other** _Doesn't exist, myth,_

This question is designed to introduce the subject of who Jesus is, which is the theme for this session. It will also give you a feel for the background of each group member (eg: whether their friends and family have particular beliefs).

BIBLE DISCUSSION

🗨 *Ask the group members to turn to Mark 2 in their Gospels, Bibles or printed sheets.*

👁 **Read aloud Mark 2:1-12**

🗨 *If your group members have English as a second language, encourage them to read the passage a second time in their own language. This will help them to understand the passage better. It will also help them if and when they return home – see page 33.*

🗨 *There is a list of Bible words from this week's passages (NIV) on pages 10-11 of the group member's Handbook. Depending on your group, it may be appropriate to go through some or all of these words at this point. The word list for this study is also shown opposite.*

Bible words

Mark 2:1-12

v1 Capernaum. A town near the Sea of Galilee. See map on page 4 (of the group member's Handbook).

v2 preached the word. Taught people the good news (the "gospel").

v3 paralytic. A person who is unable to move their legs and maybe their arms as well.

v5 faith. Trust/belief. Faith in God means trusting that God will do what he says.

v5 sins. Rebellion against God; doing what *we* want instead of what *God* wants.

v5 forgiven. Treated as if we had never sinned.

v6 teachers of the law. Jewish religious leaders. Teachers of the Jewish religious law.

v6 blaspheming. Lying about God, or claiming to have rights and powers that belong to God.

v8 knew in his spirit. Knew exactly what the religious leaders were thinking.

v10 the Son of Man. A title Jesus often used for himself.

v10 authority. The right and power to be in charge.

v12 praised God. Spoke or sang about God's greatness, and thanked him for what they had seen.

Daniel 7:13-14

v13 vision. Dream sent by God.

v14 glory. Greatness and honour.

v14 sovereign power. Power to rule as king.

v14 nations. Countries.

v14 worshipped. Thanked and praised.

👁 **Re-read Mark 2:1-12**

1. What problem did the four men have (see verses 2-4)?

They had a friend who could not walk and they wanted to bring him to Jesus. They could not reach Jesus because there were too many people in the house.

2. How did the four men solve this problem (see verse 4)?

They made a hole in the roof and lowered their friend down to Jesus.

You may want to explain that many houses in Bible times had flat roofs with stairs or a ladder leading up to them. Roofs were often covered with loose tiles or branches. These could be lifted up to make a hole.

Note: This is a great opportunity to point out to internationals that this took place in the Middle East. The Bible is not a western book, nor Christianity a western religion.

3. What did they expect Jesus to do for the paralyzed man?

They expected Jesus to heal him.

You may want to ask why the men expected Jesus to heal their friend. If appropriate, you could suggest they read Mark 1:21-34.

Alternatively you can simply explain that Jesus had become well known in Capernaum for healing the sick. He also amazed people with his teaching and his power to drive out evil spirits (Mark 1:21-34).

4. What did Jesus do (see verse 5)? Why do you think he did that?

- Jesus said to the man: "Son, your sins are forgiven".

- Jesus believed that the man's greatest need was to have his sins forgiven, not to be healed. This is because our relationship with God is more important than anything else. This means that sin is our greatest problem, because it spoils our relationship with God, and the effects of this can last for ever.

This is the first time the group have met the concepts of sin and forgiveness. Explain that they will find out more about this in the next session.

Note: Group members might ask if sin and disability are linked. If they do, explain that in other parts of the Bible Jesus says that sin is not the cause of disability or disasters. (For example, see John 9:1-3 and Luke 13:1-5.)

5. Why were the religious leaders so angry (see verses 6-7)?

Jesus was claiming to do something that only God can do – forgive sins. Sin offends God. So only God has the right to forgive it. The religious leaders knew that only God can forgive sins. So they decided that Jesus was blaspheming. They thought he was lying about being able to do the same as God.

Note: Your group members will probably have a wrong understanding of sin. Begin to discuss it, but remember that it is covered in the next session.

6. Look at the question Jesus asks in verse 9. How would you answer it? Why?

It is easier to say: "Your sins are forgiven," because that is something unseen. You can't prove whether it has happened or not. It is more difficult to say: "Get up, take your mat and walk", because you can see whether it is true or not.

If you have time, you could divide the group in two to debate Jesus' question before discussing it as a whole group.

7. Why did Jesus heal the man (see verses 10-12)?

Jesus healed the man to show people who he is and that he has authority to forgive sin (verse 10). His authority wasn't just to forgive the man's sin, but our sin as well.

📖 *Read the notes printed on page 11 of the Handbook. They say:*

> **In Mark 2:10 Jesus calls himself the "Son of Man". The prophet Daniel came from Israel 500 years before Mark. He described the son of man:**
>
> *"In my vision at night I looked, and there before me was one like a son of man, coming with the clouds of heaven ... He was given authority, glory and sovereign power; all peoples, nations and men of every language worshipped him." (Daniel 7:13-14)*

8. In your own words, how did Daniel describe the son of man?

Ask some or all of your group to tell you their answers. If they are not sure what any of the words in Daniel 7 mean, remind them that the list of Bible words on page 11 of their Handbooks will help them.

Explain that "the Son of Man" is a title Jesus often used for himself. In Daniel 7:13-14, the "son of man" looks like a man, comes "with the clouds of heaven", and is given authority to rule over everyone for ever.

You may need to explain that the quote is from the Old Testament part of the Bible, and that a prophet was a man who spoke words that came from God. The prophets spoke to the people of that time, but often they also spoke about a future event. Daniel's vision pointed to a future event.

Note: In the full passage, Daniel 7:9-14, we also see that the "son of man" came to God (the "Ancient of Days", verse 9), and that he is a King whose kingdom will never end.

9. Daniel's book was well known in Israel. What did Jesus expect people to understand when he called himself the "Son of Man" in Mark 2:10?

The people listening to Jesus – the religious leaders and the rest of the people crowded into the room – were Jewish. They would know the Old Testament well, so they would recognise the title "son of man" from Daniel's vision. Jesus expected them to understand that Daniel was writing about him – that he had been given authority by God – in this case authority to forgive sin.

10. What does this event tell us about who Jesus is?

It tells us that Jesus is someone with the same authority as God. He healed the paralyzed man, which proved that he did have authority to forgive the man's sins. This showed the people who were there – and us – that Jesus is God, since only God can forgive sins. You may like to read the end of verse 7 again: "Who can forgive sins but God alone?".

TO FINISH

Read the summary printed on page 12 of the Handbook. It says:

Jesus has power and authority to forgive sin.

Mark also shows that Jesus has power and authority:

- **to teach (see for example Mark 1:21-22)**

- **over evil spirits (see for example Mark 1:23-27)**

- **over sickness (see for example Mark 1:29-34)**

- **over nature (see for example Mark 4:35-41)**

- **and even over death (see for example Mark 5:35-42)**

The evidence in Mark's Gospel tells us that Jesus was a man with the power and authority of God himself. He is the Son of God.

CHAPTE 2 IDENTITY – 18 MINS

If you feel it is appropriate for your group, you may like to show episode 2 of the Christianity Explored *DVD at this point. The DVD can be used as a summary or a refresher for the main teaching point of this session. However, it also includes Bible passages and concepts that have not been covered in this Bible study, so please watch it in advance to judge whether or not your group members would find it helpful.*

If it's appropriate for your group, ask them to read Mark 3:13 – 5:43 before the next session. There's space at the back of the group member's Handbook, on page 37, for them to write down any questions they have. Group members will benefit from reading through Mark's Gospel while doing Christianity Explored – but this may be too much for some to attempt. It's more important that they feel able to come back to the group next time, rather than worrying that they've been unable to do their "homework".

Thank your group members for coming and encourage them to come back next time. Tell them: We've seen one of the amazing things Jesus did and said. Next time we're going to explore what Jesus said about himself.

AFTERWARDS

Did you manage to keep the focus on the big idea of this session?

Did any of the group members ask a question or make a comment that you could follow up? If so, plan how you will do that, as well as praying for that person.

Is the group talking more than you are? How can you help the quieter ones to open up a little more?

Thank God for those who came back this session, and pray that he will open their hearts to the truth about Jesus.

Why did Jesus come?

3

THE BIG IDEA

We have all sinned and face judgment. The punishment for sin is hell. Jesus came to rescue us from hell.

Ask everyone to turn to Session 3 on page 13 of the Christianity Explored Universal Handbook.

If you suggested that your group read Mark 3:7 – 5:43 at home, ask if they have any questions about what they read. The appendix on page 125 lists common questions from Mark along with suggestions for answering them.

Read the summary of Session 2, called "The story so far", on page 13 of the Handbook. It says:

- **Christianity is about Jesus Christ.**

- **It is the good news (the "gospel") about Jesus.**

- **When Jesus was baptized by John, God's voice was heard. God called Jesus his Son.**

- **When four men brought a paralyzed man to Jesus, he forgave the man's sin. Then Jesus healed the man to prove that he has the power and authority to forgive sin.**

- **Mark's Gospel shows that Jesus has the power and authority of God himself. Jesus is the Son of God.**

Explain that in this session we will find out more about why Jesus came and what he came to do.

Leader's checklist
Have you...
☐ Reminded group members where and when you will meet (eg: by email or text message)?
☐ Prepared food and drinks?
☐ Enough Gospels, Bibles or printed-out sheets with the Bible passages on them?
☐ Handbooks for each person, plus spares if needed?
☐ Thought through your answers to each of the questions?
☐ Prayed for each group member and yourself as the leader?
☐ The optional Christianity Explored DVD ready to play?

OPENING DISCUSSION QUESTION

Ask your group the following question.

What do you think is the world's biggest problem?

☐ **War**

☐ **Poverty**

☐ **Pollution**

☐ **Racism**

☐ **Greed**

☐ **Other** _____

In our last session, what was the paralyzed man's biggest problem?

These two questions are designed to introduce the idea that we all have a huge problem that needs to be solved. The theme for this session is that Jesus came to solve this problem.

BIBLE DISCUSSION

Ask the group members to turn to Mark 12 in their Gospels, Bibles or printed sheets.

Read aloud Mark 12:28-30

If your group members have English as a second language, encourage them to read the passage a second time in their own language. This will help them to understand the passage better. It will also help them if and when they return home – see page 33.

There is a list of Bible words from this week's passages (NIV) on pages 14-15 of the group member's Handbook. Depending on your group, it may be appropriate to go through some or all of these words at this point. The word list for this study is also shown opposite.

Bible words	
Mark 12:28-30	**v22 deceit.** Cheating, lying.
v28 teachers of the law. A group of Jewish religious leaders.	**v22 lewdness.** Being rude about sexual things.
v28 debating. Discussing, arguing.	**v22 envy.** Wanting what belongs to other people.
v28 commandments. Instructions, rules. The "Ten Commandments" were given by God to show his rescued people how to live.	**v22 slander.** Telling lies about someone.
v29 "Hear, O Israel". A command telling the Israelites to listen to God.	**v22 arrogance.** Pride. Thinking you are better or more clever than others.
v29 Lord. Master or leader.	**v22 folly.** Foolishness.
v30 heart, soul, mind, strength. Every part of you.	**Mark 9:43-47**
Mark 7:20-23	**v43 sin.** Doing what we want instead of what God wants. Sin is rebellion against God.
v20 unclean. Dirty in God's sight. If someone was "unclean", they could not enter the temple in Jerusalem.	**v43 maimed.** Permanently injured.
	v44 hell. Being separated from God, and from everything that is good, for ever.
v21 sexual immorality. Any sexual thoughts or actions that are not part of marriage.	**v44 crippled.** Disabled.
v21 adultery. Sex with a person who is married to someone else.	**v47 pluck.** Pull or pick out.
v22 malice. Doing something to deliberately harm someone else.	**v47 the kingdom of God.** God's kingdom isn't a place. It is God's people living with him as their King now and for ever.

👁 **Re-read Mark 12:28-30**

1. How should we treat God (see verse 30)?

We should love the Lord our God with all our heart and with all our soul and with all our mind and with all our strength.

God made us, gives us every good thing we enjoy, and has power and authority over our lives. Jesus tells us that our response should be to love God.

• You may want to ask your group: **Which part of this command sounds most challenging? Why?**

The really challenging word here is "all" – love God with *all* your heart, soul, mind and strength. So no part of our lives should be held back from God. He is to have all of everything. This includes how we think, what our hopes are, what we do with our bodies, how we spend our time, what we treat as important, etc.

2. How do we treat God?

We do not love God with all our heart, all our soul, all our mind and all our strength. In other words, we do not love God with every part of us.

We decide exactly what we will do with our heart, soul, mind and strength. And instead of loving God, we live as if we were God.

Note: Some of your group may ask what the soul is. This is actually a theologically complex question, but we suggest you keep it simple by explaining that your soul is your spirit. When Jesus referred to our heart, soul, mind and strength in verse 30, he was referring to every part of us, everything that makes us the people we are.

Internationals: Loving God more than your family is a shocking idea if you come from an Asian or African culture where family loyalty (filial piety) is one of the greatest values in society. If you get into a discussion on this, it is worth pointing out that Jesus also expected his followers to honour their father and mother (eg: Mark 10:18-19).

🔲 *Read the notes printed on page 14 of the Handbook. They say:*

None of us has loved God as we should. Instead of loving God, we have all turned away from him.

We have all rebelled against God by doing what *we* want instead of what *he* wants. This is called sin.

🔲 *If appropriate for your group, you may want to use the illustration of family relationships:*

Parents are usually very kind and generous to their children, making big sacrifices for them – for example, in providing a good education. Some parents make financial sacrifices so that their children can go on a school trip or even study abroad. It would be a terrible and shameful thing for children to take all these gifts but then cut themselves off from their parents, refusing even to speak to them.

This is how we have all behaved towards God. We are happy to take the gifts that he gives us – life, health, family, friends and so on. But we refuse to acknowledge that it is God who has given the gifts, and we ignore him completely. This is called sin.

👁 Read aloud Mark 7:20-23

📋 *Note: Christianity Explored is based on the 1984 version of the New International Version (NIV). If you are using the 2011 revised NIV, you will find that "unclean" in verses 20 and 23 has been changed to "defiled". This is another way of explaining that being "unclean" meant you were dirty in God's sight and unfit to enter the temple.*

📋 *If your group members have English as a second language, encourage them to read the passage a second time in their own language.*

📋 *Depending on your group, it may be appropriate to go through some or all of the Bible words listed on pages 14-15 of the Handbook at this point. The word list for this study is also shown on page 29 of this Leader's Guide.*

👁 Re-read Mark 7:20-23

3. Where does sin come from (see verses 21 and 23)?

Sin comes from within, from our hearts. We all have a heart problem: out of our hearts come the evils listed in verses 21-22.

You may want to ask your group if this surprises them.

4. What is the result of our sin (see verses 20 and 23)?

It makes us "unclean" in God's eyes. Because God is clean, holy and pure, our sin makes us dirty – "unclean" (that is, unacceptable) – to him. Our uncleanness means we have a broken relationship with God.

📋 *Read the notes printed on page 15 of the Handbook. They say:*

The evils that come out of our hearts make us "unclean". They keep us away from God because he is completely pure and good.

God will not ignore our sin – it must be punished.

Sin is our greatest problem.

👁 Read aloud Mark 9:43-47

Note: Christianity Explored is based on the 1984 version of the New International Version (NIV). If you are using the 2011 revised NIV, you will find that "sin" has been changed to "stumble" each time. "Stumble" is probably a better translation of the Greek than "sin". But explain that Jesus doesn't mean accidental stumbling, but actual sin which causes a moral fall.

If your group members have English as a second language, encourage them to read the passage a second time in their own language.

Depending on your group, it may be appropriate to go through some or all of the Bible words listed on page 15 of the Handbook at this point. The word list for this study is also shown on page 29 of this Leader's Guide.

👁 Re-read Mark 9:43-47

5. What does Jesus tell us to do about the causes of sin?

Jesus tells us to "cut them off" – to get rid of them completely.

Ask your group: **If we did this, why would we still have a problem?**

In question 3 we saw that, according to Jesus, our problem is not our hands, or feet or eyes – but our *hearts* (Mark 7:20-23). We cannot cut out our hearts, so we are powerless to help ourselves. We need the rescue that only Jesus can provide.

6. Why do you think Jesus uses such serious examples when talking about the need to avoid hell?

• Because hell is a terrible place of eternal punishment. It means being separated from God, and from everything that is good, for ever.

• The reason Jesus warns us about hell is because he loves us and does not want us to go there.

Hell is so serious that Jesus uses extreme examples to make his point. It we find them too extreme, it's probably because we underestimate the seriousness of the heart problem Jesus talks about in Mark 7:20-23.

Note: Jesus did not intend that a person should physically cut off a hand or foot, or pluck out an eye. Jesus is making the point that if anything is stopping us from entering the kingdom of God, we need to get rid of it. It is better to take drastic action to rid ourselves of it, whatever it is, than end up in hell for ever.

7. Jesus believed in hell. Should we? Why or why not?

In the 21st century many western people either dismiss hell as a made-up story, or make jokes about it. For many internationals, however, the concept of hell is very strong and something that is deeply feared.

Whichever view your group members have, they need to understand that Jesus was very serious about the reality and horror of hell.

He lovingly warns us so that we can be rescued from hell, a threat he took so seriously that he was ready to die to save us from it. (Explain that we'll be exploring Jesus' death in more detail next time.)

Note: The appendix on page 134 gives help in answering questions about hell.

8. What would you say if someone said to you: "When I die, God will be pleased with me because I am a good person"?

Encourage your group to answer this from what they have learned today.

• There is no such thing as a "good person". Nobody has loved God with all their heart. No one has lived with him at the centre of his or her life.

• We all have a heart problem: out of our hearts come the evils listed in Mark 7:21-22.

• A person may seem to be living a good life but still have a sinful heart and live in rebellion against Jesus Christ. It is this rebellion (which the Bible calls sin) that angers God. The punishment for it is hell.

TO FINISH

Read the summary printed on page 16 of the Handbook. It says:

• **We have all sinned – we have rebelled against God.**

• **We are all unclean – we face his punishment.**

• **We all need to be forgiven – we need to be rescued.**

That is why Jesus came.

Jesus said: "It is not the healthy who need a doctor, but the sick. I have not come to call the righteous, but sinners" (Mark 2:17).

Jesus came to rescue us from hell, the punishment our sin deserves, and to bring us into his kingdom. In the next session we will learn how he does that.

CHAPTER3 - SIN 14 MINS

- *If you feel it is appropriate for your group, you may like to show episode 3 of the* Christianity Explored *DVD at this point. The DVD can be used as a summary or a refresher for the main teaching point of this session. However, it also includes Bible passages and concepts that have not been covered in this Bible study, so please watch it in advance to judge whether or not your group members would find it helpful.*

- *If it's appropriate for your group, ask them to read Mark 6:1 – 8:29 before the next session. There's space at the back of the group member's Handbook, on page 38, for them to write down any questions they have. Group members will benefit from reading through Mark's Gospel while doing* Christianity Explored – *but this may be too much for some to attempt. It's more important that they feel able to come back to the group next time rather than worrying that they've been unable to do their "homework".*

- *Thank your group members for coming and encourage them to come back next time. Tell them:* We've seen that our biggest problem is sin, and that the punishment for sin is hell. Next time we're going to explore why Jesus died, and how his death can rescue us from our sin.

AFTERWARDS

- Did you manage to keep the focus on the big idea of this session ie: that we have all sinned and face judgment, and that Jesus came to rescue us from hell, the punishment our sin deserves?

- Did any of the group members ask a question or make a comment that you could follow up? If so, plan how you will do that, as well as praying for that person.

- Is the group talking more than you are? How can you help the quieter ones to open up a little more?

- Thank God for each group member, and pray that he will open their hearts to the truth about who Jesus is and why he came.

Why did Jesus die?

4

THE BIG IDEA

When Jesus died on the cross, he took on himself our sin and God's punishment for our sin. He died to rescue us from God's judgment.

📺 *Ask everyone to turn to Session 4 on page 17 of the Christianity Explored Universal Handbook.*

📺 *If you suggested that your group read Mark 6:1 – 8:29 at home, ask if they have any questions about what they read. The appendix on page 125 lists common questions from Mark along with suggestions for answering them.*

📺 *Read the summary of Session 3, called "The story so far", on page 17 of the Handbook. It says:*

- **Christianity is about Jesus Christ. It is the good news (the "gospel") about Jesus.**

- **Jesus is the Son of God. He has the power and authority of God himself. This includes the power and authority to forgive sin.**

- **We have all sinned – we have rebelled against God.**

- **We all face God's punishment. We all need to be forgiven – we need to be rescued.**

- **Jesus came to rescue us from hell, the punishment our sin deserves.**

📺 *Explain that in this session we will find out why Jesus died and why his death was the only way to rescue us.*

Leader's checklist

Have you…

- ☐ Reminded group members where and when you will meet (eg: by email or text message)?

- ☐ Prepared food and drinks?

- ☐ Enough Gospels, Bibles or printed-out sheets with the Bible passages on them?

- ☐ Handbooks for each person, plus spares if needed?

- ☐ Thought through your answers to each of the questions?

- ☐ Prayed for each group member and yourself as the leader?

- ☐ The optional Christianity Explored DVD ready to play?

OPENING DISCUSSION QUESTION

📖 *Ask your group the following question.*

Where do you see crosses today?

📖 *Read the notes printed on page 17 of the Handbook. They say:*

In Jesus' day, people were punished by being nailed to a wooden cross and left to die. It was terrible and shameful to die in this way.

God spoke about this kind of punishment hundreds of years before when he said: "Anyone who is hung on a tree is under God's curse" (Deuteronomy 21:23).

Mark's Gospel tells us that Jesus predicted his own death three times (Mark 8:31, 9:30-31, 10:32-34). He said that this "must" happen.

This question, and the notes that follow it, are designed to help your group think about where and how crosses are used today, and then to understand what dying on a cross meant 2000 years ago.

Note: If appropriate for your group and if you have time, you could ask them to read some or all of the passages above: Mark 8:31, 9:30-31, 10:32-34. You could also ask them to make a list of all the things Jesus said must and would happen.

BIBLE DISCUSSION

📖 *Ask the group members to turn to Mark 15 in their Gospels, Bibles or printed sheets.*

👁 Read aloud Mark 15:33-39

📖 *If your group members have English as a second language, encourage them to read the passage a second time in their own language. This will help them to understand the passage better. It will also help them if and when they return home – see page 33.*

📖 *There is a list of Bible words from this week's passages (NIV) on pages 18-19 of the group member's Handbook. Depending on your group, it may be appropriate to go through some or all of these words at this point. The word list for this study is also shown opposite.*

Bible words	
Mark 15:33-39 **v33 the sixth hour.** 12.00 pm, mid-day. **v33 the ninth hour.** 3.00 pm, mid-afternoon. **v34 "Eloi, Eloi, lama sabachthani?"** Jesus was speaking in the Aramaic language. It means: "My God, my God, why have you forsaken me?" **v34 forsaken.** Abandoned, left. **v35 Elijah.** An important prophet (messenger from God) in the Old Testament. **v36 sponge.** Something that soaks up (absorbs) liquid.	**v36 wine vinegar.** Vinegar made from wine. **v36 offered.** Held out, gave. **v37 a loud cry.** A loud shout. **v37 breathed his last.** Stopped breathing. Died. **v38 temple.** The Jewish temple in Jerusalem. **v39 centurion.** Roman army officer. **v39 surely.** Certainly, for sure.
	Mark 10:45 **v45 the Son of Man.** A title (name) Jesus often used about himself. **v45 ransom.** A price paid to buy back and/or free a slave.

👁 **Re-read Mark 15:33**

1. What unusual event happened at mid-day (the "sixth hour") as Jesus was dying?

Mark is counting hours using the Jewish system, so the sixth hour would have been 12.00 pm, noon. The mid-day sun should have been at its brightest in the sky, but darkness fell over the whole land and remained until 3.00 pm in the afternoon.

You may like to ask your group if there is a natural explanation for this.

Jesus died at Passover time (when Jewish people remember how God rescued them from slavery in Egypt). This means the darkness could not have been an eclipse, because Passover always happens on a full moon and a solar eclipse is impossible during a full moon. During a full moon, the moon is here:

Sun

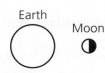
Earth   Moon

But, for an eclipse to occur, the moon would have to be here:

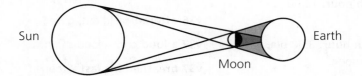

so that it can cast its shadow between the sun and the earth.

Also, solar eclipses never last more than about six minutes. This darkness lasted for three hours.

So, something supernatural was happening.

2. In the Bible, darkness is a sign of God's anger and judgment. What is surprising about the focus of God's anger here?

God's anger is focused on Jesus. But Jesus had never sinned; he led a sinless life. So it is surprising that Jesus should be the focus of God's anger and judgment.

The Father's anger for the sin of his people was poured out on his Son.

Note: Amos 5:20; 8:9, Exodus 10:21-23 and Isaiah 13:9-10 give examples of darkness as a sign of God's anger in the Old Testament.

📖 *Read the note printed on page 18 of the Handbook. It says:*

God punished Jesus, so that we don't have to be punished.

3. What was the relationship between Jesus and his Father before his death on the cross? (See Mark 1:9-11 and Mark 9:7.)

God the Father and God the Son had always enjoyed a perfect relationship of love. At Jesus' baptism, and when he appeared in glory on the mountain, God the Father said he was pleased with his Son and loved him. This shows us that Jesus had never sinned.

👁 **Re-read Mark 15:34**

4. What happened between Jesus and his Father at the cross?

Jesus was abandoned (forsaken) by his Father. He cried out: "My God, my God, why have you forsaken me?" On the cross Jesus was abandoned by God.

Explain why Jesus was abandoned by God by making the following points:

- When Jesus died on the cross, he carried our sin and suffered God's judgment in our place. God cannot tolerate sin so he turned away from his own Son.

- God's judgment fell on Jesus because he was taking upon himself all the punishment that our sin deserves. Jesus died as our substitute, taking the punishment we deserve for our sin. He died in our place.

- Jesus paid the price for sin so that we never have to. He died for the sin of everyone who puts their trust in him.

Note: You may want to explain the idea of substitution: "In many games of sport, one player will be taken out of the game and another sent in their place. This new player is the substitute. When Jesus died, he took our place in facing God's judgment for our sin. He is our substitute."

📖 *Read the note printed on page 18 of the Handbook. It says:*

Jesus chose to be abandoned so that we do not have to be.

👁 **Re-read Mark 15:37-38**

5. What happened in the temple in Jerusalem when Jesus died?

The curtain in the temple was torn in two from top to bottom.

Note: If a person tore the curtain, they would naturally hold the bottom of it and tear it from the bottom to the top. But the curtain was torn from top to bottom, because it was torn by God.

📖 *Read the note printed on page 19 of the Handbook, and look at the diagram that shows the position of the curtain. The note says:*

Sinful people cannot meet with God, because he is holy.

The curtain in the middle of the temple stopped sinful people from meeting with God in the Most Holy Place (see picture).

Only once a year, a priest was able to go through the curtain and meet with God in the Most Holy Place. But the priest could only do that after he made special sacrifices.

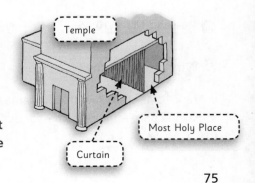

Note: Before looking at question 6, you may want to ask: **What changed when the curtain in the temple was torn?** This may help your group members to understand question 6 more clearly.

6. How did Jesus' death change our relationship with God?

You might want to use this illustration: "In some theatres, during the interval a fire curtain is drawn across the stage. This stops people getting onto the stage and, if there is a fire on stage, the curtain protects the audience from danger. In a similar way, the temple curtain stopped people getting into the Most Holy Place, and protected the people from God's holiness."

In Mark 15:37-38, Mark suddenly stops telling us what's happening at the cross and takes us to the temple in Jerusalem. He does this to explain the result of Jesus' death for us. The temple curtain was like a big "No entry" sign. It said loudly and clearly that it is impossible for sinful people like you and me to meet with God.

Then suddenly, as Jesus died on the cross, God tore this curtain in two, from top to bottom. He did this to show that the way is now open for people to come near to him. And that's only possible because Jesus has paid the price for our sin.

Read the note printed on page 19 of the Handbook. It says:

We can be accepted by God because Jesus died for us.

The way to God is now open.

Read aloud Mark 10:45

If your group members have English as a second language, encourage them to read the passage a second time in their own language.

Depending on your group, it may be appropriate to go through some or all of the Bible words listed on page 19 of the Handbook at this point. The word list for this study is also shown on page 37 of this Leader's Guide.

Re-read Mark 10:45

7. Why did Jesus die?

In Mark 10:45 Jesus says that he came to serve us. He did this by dying in our place to pay the price – the ransom – for our sin. He paid the price so that we never have to.

You may want to explain to the group that the "ransom" Jesus talks about wasn't money paid to a kidnapper. In those days a slave could be given their freedom if a "ransom" was paid.

Encourage your group also to answer this question from what they have learned in the rest of this session. Phrases they might use include: "to take the punishment for our sin", "to rescue us from God's judgment", "to open the way for us to come to God".

📖 *Read the note printed on page 20 of the Handbook. It says:*

Jesus died in our place to pay the price – the ransom – for our sin.

8. What is your reaction to this?

This question is designed to help group members think about what this means for them personally.

It will also help you to understand where they have got to in their thinking. Some answers may also show that someone hasn't fully understood the teaching in this session, in which case this is a good time to go over it again.

TO FINISH

📖 *Read the summary printed on page 20 of the Handbook. It says:*

Jesus was punished – instead of us.

Jesus chose to be abandoned – so that we do not have to be.

Jesus died as a ransom – to pay the price for our sin.

As Jesus died, the curtain in the temple was torn in two from top to bottom.
This shows that we can be accepted by God because Jesus died for us. The way to God is now open.

📖 *Use the illustration on the next page to help your group understand what happened when Jesus died.*

What to do	What to say

Hold up a blank DVD case in your right hand.

Imagine that this DVD contains the whole of your life. It shows everything you have ever done, said and thought.

There are a lot of things on here that look great to us. Perhaps there's a loving home, kind actions, achievements and success. But there is also a lot on this DVD that you're ashamed of. Things you'd prefer people not to see. We all have secrets that we don't want others to know about.

The Bible says:

> *"Nothing God created is hidden from him. His eyes see everything. He will hold us accountable for everything we do."* (Hebrews 4:13, NIrV)

This DVD doesn't just show the way we've treated others, but also the way we've treated God.

Hold your left hand out, with your palm facing the ceiling.

Now imagine that my left hand is me, and the ceiling is God. Between God and me is all of my sin, and it separates me from God.

Take the DVD and put it flat on your hand.

My sin cuts me off from God. It gets in the way between him and me. But let me show you what happened as Jesus died on the cross.

What to do	**What to say**

Hold out your right hand, facing up. Your left hand should still have the DVD.

Imagine that my right hand is Jesus – and remember that the ceiling is God. Jesus lived a sinless life. He never sinned. He always perfectly obeyed God – so there was nothing separating him from God.

But Jesus said that he came to "give his life as a ransom for many". So when he was on the cross, he took my sin. He paid the ransom price for my sin.

Now transfer the DVD from the left hand to the right hand.

That's why Jesus cried out: *"My God, my God, why have you forsaken me?"* as he hung on the cross. It wasn't his sin that separated him from God, because Jesus had never sinned. No, it was *our* sin that made him feel abandoned by God.

Jesus took upon himself all the punishment that our sin, everything on this DVD, deserves. He chose to be our substitute, taking the punishment we deserve.

Refer to your left hand, now empty, still facing upwards.

How much sin is left? *(Wait for an answer – don't worry if it's a long pause. That will make the point even more clearly.)* Yes that's right, nothing.

Jesus' death means we can be accepted by God. Jesus paid the price for our sin.

The amazing truth is that Jesus loved us enough to die for our sin and rescue everyone who puts their trust in him.

If you feel it is appropriate for your group, you may like to show episode 4 of the Christianity Explored *DVD at this point. The DVD can be used as a summary or a refresher for the main teaching point of this session. However, it also includes Bible passages and concepts that have not been covered in this Bible study, so please watch it in advance to judge whether or not your group members would find it helpful.*

If it's appropriate for your group, ask them to read Mark 8:30 – 10:52 before the next session. There's space at the back of the group member's Handbook, on page 38, for them to write down any questions they have. Group members will benefit from reading through Mark's Gospel while doing Christianity Explored *– but this may be too much for some to attempt. It's more important that they feel able to come back to the group next time rather than worrying that they've been unable to do their "homework".*

Thank your group members for coming and encourage them to come back next time. Tell them: We've seen that Jesus died to rescue us from the punishment our sin deserves. But the Bible tells us that Jesus didn't stay dead. So next time we will explore why Jesus rose from the dead.

AFTERWARDS

Did you manage to keep the focus on the big idea of this session – that Jesus died to take the punishment for our sin and rescue us from God's judgment?

Did any of the group members ask a question or make a comment that you could follow up? If so, plan how you will do that, as well as praying for that person.

Thank God for each group member, and pray that he will open their hearts to the truth about why Jesus died.

Why did Jesus rise from the dead?

THE BIG IDEA

Two days after he died, Jesus rose from the dead, just as he said he would. Everything that Jesus said would happen did happen.

▣ *Ask everyone to turn to Session 5 on page 21 of the Christianity Explored Universal Handbook.*

▣ *If you suggested that your group read Mark 8:30 – 10:52 at home, ask if they have any questions about what they read. The appendix on page 125 lists common questions from Mark along with suggestions for answering them.*

▣ *Read the summary of Session 4, called "The story so far", on page 21 of the Handbook. It says:*

- **Christianity is about Jesus Christ. It is the good news (the "gospel") about Jesus.**

- **Jesus is the Son of God. He has the power and authority of God himself. This includes the power and authority to forgive sin.**

- **We have all sinned – we have rebelled against God.**

- **We all face God's punishment. We all need to be forgiven – we need to be rescued.**

- **Jesus came to rescue us from hell, the punishment our sin deserves.**

- **God punished Jesus, so that we don't have to be punished. Jesus died on a cross as a ransom, to pay the price for our sin.**

- **We can be accepted by God because Jesus died for us.**

Leader's checklist

Have you...

- ☐ Reminded group members where and when you will meet (eg: by email or text message)?
- ☐ Prepared food and drinks?
- ☐ Enough Gospels, Bibles or printed-out sheets with the Bible passages on them?
- ☐ Handbooks for each person, plus spares if needed?
- ☐ Thought through your answers to each of the questions?
- ☐ Prayed for each group member and yourself as the leader?
- ☐ The optional Christianity Explored DVD ready to play?

🔲 Explain that in this session we will find out what happened after Jesus died and why the resurrection matters.

OPENING DISCUSSION QUESTION

🔲 Ask your group the following question.

What do you think happens to us after we die?

This question is designed to help your group think about their own understanding of death and what happens afterwards. It will also help you to know what issues may need to be talked about during this session.

For example, if some in your group believe that people are reincarnated after death, then you will want to make it clear that resurrection is not the same as reincarnation. Reincarnation is a new life in this world, and would eventually lead to death again. Resurrection is a new life in God's perfect new heaven and earth, and with a new and perfect body.

Note: Don't get sidetracked into a long discussion about the various beliefs people may have about what happens after we die. The purpose of this question is simply to introduce the subject.

BIBLE DISCUSSION

🔲 Ask the group members to turn to Mark 15 in their Gospels, Bibles or printed sheets.

👁 **Read aloud Mark 15:42-47**

🔲 If your group members have English as a second language, encourage them to read the passage a second time in their own language. This will help them to understand the passage better. It will also help them if and when they return home – see page 33.

🔲 There is a list of Bible words from this week's passages (NIV) on pages 22-23 of the group member's Handbook. Depending on your group, it may be appropriate to go through some or all of these words at this point. The word list for this study is also shown opposite.

Bible words	
Mark 15:42-47	**v46 entrance.** Way in, opening.
v42 Preparation Day. The day before the Sabbath.	**Mark 16:1-8**
v42 Sabbath. Jewish holy day. The Sabbath lasts from sunset on Friday to sunset on Saturday.	**v1 anoint Jesus' body.** Put oil or spices on the body of Jesus.
	v2 first day of the week. Sunday.
v42 approached. Came near.	**v5 robe.** Long piece of clothing.
v43 Arimathea. A town in the south of Israel.	**v5 alarmed.** Scared, frightened.
v43 prominent. Important.	**v6 Nazarene.** Someone from Nazareth, a town in the north of Israel (see the map on page 4).
v43 the Council. Important group of Jewish leaders.	
v43 waiting for the kingdom of God. Waiting for God to send his chosen King to lead his people.	**v6 crucified.** Nailed to a cross and left to die.
	v6 risen. Come to life again.
v43 boldly. Bravely.	**v6 laid him.** Put him down.
v43 Pilate. The Roman governor in charge of Israel.	**v7 disciples.** Followers.
	v7 Galilee. The north part of Israel. See the map on page 4.
v44 summoning. Sending for.	
v45 centurion. Roman army officer.	**v8 trembling.** Shaking.
v46 linen. Type of material/cloth.	**v8 bewildered.** Puzzled, confused.
v46 tomb. Cave cut out of the rocky hillside to bury a body in.	**v8 fled.** Ran away.

👁 **Re-read Mark 15:42-47**

1. How did Pilate, the Roman governor, know that Jesus was dead (see verses 44-45)?

He asked the Roman centurion who had been in charge of the crucifixion – see Mark 15:39. This centurion would have been an experienced soldier, and had probably been involved in crucifixions before. He would have known for certain that Jesus was dead.

The centurion would have made sure that he gave the correct answer because he was being asked by Pilate, the powerful Roman governor.

2. Where was Jesus buried (see verse 46)?

In a tomb cut out of rock (ie: cut into a rocky hillside). The tomb was then sealed by rolling a large stone in front of the entrance.

Note: We know a bit more about the tomb from the other Gospels. Matthew 27:60 says that this was Joseph of Arimathea's own tomb, newly cut – presumably to be ready for him or others from his family when they died. Family tombs were often used for more than one body, but Luke 23:53 tells us that no one had yet been laid in this tomb.

👁 Read aloud Mark 16:1-8

If your group members have English as a second language, encourage them to read the passage a second time in their own language.

Depending on your group, it may be appropriate to go through some or all of the Bible words listed on page 23 of the Handbook at this point. The word list for this study is also shown on page 47 of this Leader's Guide.

👁 Re-read Mark 16:1-8

3. Why did the women go to Jesus' tomb (see verse 1)?

They went to anoint Jesus' body with spices. This meant putting spices onto the dead body.

You could ask your group: **Do you know why the women wanted to do this?**

• Bodies were treated in this way to stop them from decaying and rotting, which would cause a very bad smell.

• Jesus had been buried quickly (because the Sabbath was about to begin – see Mark 15:42 and Luke 23:54 – and no work was allowed on the Sabbath). There has been no time to put spices on the body.

Note: It's clear that the women expected to find a dead body that needed to be treated with the spices. They were not expecting Jesus to have risen from the dead.

4. What were they thinking about as they went to the tomb (see verses 2-3)?

They were wondering who would roll away the large stone that was blocking the entrance to the tomb.

5. What did they find when they got to the tomb (see verses 4-6)?

- The stone had been rolled away.

- Inside the tomb they saw a young man dressed in a white robe.

- The tomb was empty. Jesus' body was not there.

- The young man in the empty tomb tells them the reason why Jesus' body is not there: "He has risen!" (verse 6). The tomb was empty because Jesus isn't dead any more. He is alive.

Note: Mark doesn't tell us the identity of this "young man" – though he is clearly a messenger from God. If your group asks, you can tell them that Matthew 28:2 describes this messenger as "an angel of the Lord". "Angel" means "messenger".

6. The empty tomb should not have surprised the women. Why not? (See verse 7 and Mark 14:28.)

- Jesus had told them several times that he would rise from the dead and they would see him again.

- They'd forgotten, ignored or misunderstood what Jesus had told them would happen. In verse 7 the young man says: "Go, tell his disciples and Peter, 'He is going ahead of you into Galilee. There you will see him, just as he told you.'" This is exactly what Jesus said in Mark 14:28. (Note: If your group asks why the young man's message includes "and Peter", explain that it's because Peter hadn't believed what else Jesus said in Mark 14 – see Mark 14:27-31.)

Jesus was always in control. He knew exactly how he would die, and what would happen to him after death. And he explained everything to his followers before it happened. By now, the women should have learned to trust everything Jesus said. And so should we.

Read the note printed on page 22 of the Handbook. It says:

Jesus told his followers that he would rise from the dead. He said they would see him again.

7. In the following verses, what did Jesus say he came to do?

- **Mark 8:31**   Suffer, be rejected, die and rise again.

- **Mark 9:30-31**   Die and rise again.

- **Mark 10:32-34**   Die and rise again.

These three passages include some phrases that your group may not understand:

- "Son of Man" is a title (name) Jesus often used about himself.

- "the elders, chief priests and teachers of the law" were three groups of Jewish religious leaders.

- "after three days" is the Jewish way of counting days. The day you start is counted as the first day. So the day Jesus died was a Friday (the first day), and he rose from the dead on the Sunday (the third day).

📖 *Read the note printed on page 23 of the Handbook. It says:*

Jesus said he would suffer, be rejected and die. Three times Jesus said he would rise from the dead.

8. Why did Jesus have to die and rise again? (See Mark 10:45.)

- Jesus came to serve us, to save us from our sin.

- He gave his life as the ransom price to pay God's penalty for our sins and set us free.

9. What does the resurrection show us about Jesus?

The resurrection:

- shows us that Jesus is alive today.

- shows us that what Jesus said would happen did happen.

- gives us good reason to believe that everything else Jesus said was true.

- proves who Jesus is – the Christ, the Son of God.

No-one else has ever risen from the dead and remained alive. But Jesus said three times that this would happen – and it did. The resurrection shows that Jesus has power and authority over death – not just over his own, but also over ours.

Jesus died and rose again. We know from the rest of the Bible that Christians will also die and rise again to be with God for ever.

💬 *You may like to use this illustration to explain the difference between Jesus and someone who was brought back to life but eventually died again (eg: Jairus' daughter, Mark 5:21-24, 35-43). This can be illustrated by holding up a "box of death". Show visually that Jairus' daughter entered it; then Jesus pulled her back out of it the same way she came in; only to die again later. But when Jesus died, he entered it and went out through the other side into eternal life – the first full and true resurrection.*

Note: If your group ask about Mark 16:9-20 explain that most experts agree that Mark's Gospel ends at chapter 16:8. The women run away terrified, not knowing what to think after being told that Jesus is risen. The ending prompts the question: Are you able to see who Jesus is, why he came, and what it means to follow him?

Verses 9-20 of Mark chapter 16 appear to be attempts by later writers to add a fuller resurrection ending to Mark. However, the oldest manuscripts do not include this section and its style and vocabulary are different from the rest of Mark. This does not mean that what is contained in this ending is made up. Most of the details also appear in the other Gospels. It just means that they were probably not in Mark's original.

TO FINISH

💬 *Read the summary printed on page 24 of the Handbook. It says:*

Jesus died and was buried in a tomb cut out of rock. He died to pay the price for our sin. Jesus took the punishment we deserve.

Two days after he died, Jesus rose from the dead, just as he said he would.
His resurrection shows that he has power and authority over death – not just over his own death, but over ours as well.

Jesus died and rose again. We know from the rest of the Bible that Christians will also die and rise again.
Everyone who puts their trust in Jesus will rise again to be with God for ever.

Note: Jesus died on a Friday (often known as Good Friday) and rose from the dead on Sunday. The summary in the Handbook describes this as "Two days after he died". However, your group may ask why they have heard the resurrection described as being "On the third day" or "Three days later". If they ask, explain that this was the Jewish way of counting time. The Friday Jesus died was seen as the "first day", and so the Sunday when he rose again was called the "third day".

CHAPTER 5 – RESURECTION –15 MINS

- *If you feel it is appropriate for your group, you may like to show episode 5 of the* Christianity Explored *DVD at this point. The DVD can be used as a summary or a refresher for the main teaching point of this session. However, it also includes Bible passages and concepts that have not been covered in this Bible study, so please watch it in advance to judge whether or not your group members would find it helpful.*

- *If it's appropriate for your group, ask them to read Mark 11:1 – 13:37 before the next session. There's space at the back of the group member's Handbook, on page 39, for them to write down any questions they have.*

- *Thank your group members for coming and encourage them to come back next time. Tell them:* We've seen that Jesus died to pay the price for sin, and then rose again from the dead. Next time we're going to explore why Jesus' death and resurrection mean that sinful people can be accepted by God.

AFTERWARDS

- Did you manage to keep the focus on the big idea of this session? ie: that Jesus rose from the dead, just as he said he would, and that everything Jesus said would happen did happen.

- Did any of the group members ask a question or make a comment that you could follow up? If so, plan how you will do that, as well as praying for that person.

- Thank God for each group member, and pray that he will open their hearts to the truth about who Jesus is and why he came.

How can God accept us?

6

THE BIG IDEA

We cannot earn God's forgiveness and eternal life by doing good things. We need to come to Jesus like little children, and put our trust in him. This is grace – an undeserved gift from God. This is why God can accept us.

▸ *Ask everyone to turn to Session 6 on page 25 of the Christianity Explored Universal Handbook.*

▸ *If you suggested that your group read Mark 11:1 – 13:37 at home, ask if they have any questions about what they read. The appendix on page 125 lists common questions from Mark along with suggestions for answering them.*

▸ *Read the summary of Session 5, called "The story so far", on page 25 of the Handbook. It says:*

- **Christianity is about Jesus Christ. It is the good news (the "gospel") about Jesus.**

- **Jesus is the Son of God. He has the power and authority of God himself.**

- **We have all sinned. We all face God's punishment. We all need to be forgiven.**

- **Jesus came to rescue us from hell, the punishment our sin deserves.**

- **God punished Jesus for our sin. Jesus died on a cross as a ransom, to pay the price for our sin.**

- **Jesus rose from the dead, just as he said he would.**

- **Everyone who puts their trust in Jesus will rise again to be with God for ever.**

Leader's checklist

Have you…

☐ Reminded group members where and when you will meet (eg: by email or text message)?

☐ Prepared food and drinks?

☐ Enough Gospels, Bibles or printed-out sheets with the Bible passages on them?

☐ Handbooks for each person, plus spares if needed?

☐ Thought through your answers to each of the questions?

☐ Prayed for each group member and yourself as the leader?

☐ The optional Christianity Explored DVD ready to play?

Explain that in this session we will find out why God can accept us, even though we have all sinned and rebelled against him.

OPENING DISCUSSION QUESTION

Ask your group the following question.

If you died today, why should God give you eternal life?

Note: You may need to explain that eternal life means life with God both now and for ever.

Do not ask group members to read their answers aloud. Instead use the following illustration. You will need to have each of the answers below written out in big, lower-case letters on separate pieces of paper. Hold each one up as you read them.

Perhaps your answer is about who you are, or what you have done. Maybe you wrote something like: God should give me eternal life because...

- I do not steal
- I do not lie
- I have never killed anyone
- I am a good person
- I go to church
- I do good things
- I have been baptized
- I pray and read the Bible

(Depending on your group, you may want to replace some of these with ideas that relate to their background, eg: "I look after my family", "I'm a vegetarian", "I work for a charity"...)

They sound like good answers. But none of these things is of any use at all when it comes to being given eternal life.

There is nothing wrong with those things in themselves. It is good when people try to live honest, caring lives. But the good things we do will not give us eternal life because they cannot solve the problem of our sin.

As we will see in this session, trusting in who we are or what we have done is useless. Any answers that begins: "God should give me eternal life because **I**…" will do us no good at all.

⊡ *Collect all the pieces of paper with the wrong answers.*

⊡ *If it will be helpful for your group, you could reinforce the teaching point by ripping up the pieces of paper to show that these things are no good. But don't do this if it will be a distraction, and see the note below about working with internationals.*

Internationals: The action of ripping up their answers without any discussion is likely to hamper the willingness of internationals to share what they think on other questions, and may cause offence, so don't do it. Instead, simply collect the pieces of paper and put them to one side.

BIBLE DISCUSSION

⊡ *Ask the group members to turn to Mark 10 in their Gospels, Bibles or printed sheets.*

👁 Read aloud Mark 10:17-22

⊡ *If your group members have English as a second language, encourage them to read the passage a second time in their own language. This will help them to understand the passage better. It will also help them if and when they return home – see page 33.*

⊡ *There is a list of Bible words from this week's passages (NIV) on pages 26-27 of the group member's Handbook. Depending on your group, it may be appropriate to go through some or all of these words at this point. The word list for this study is also shown on the next page.*

Bible words	
Mark 10:17-22	**Mark 12:28-30**
v17 inherit. Receive, be given. A person may inherit something when a member of their family dies.	**v28 teachers of the law.** A group of Jewish religious leaders.
	v28 debating. Discussing, arguing.
v17 eternal life. Life with God both now and for ever.	**v29 "Hear, O Israel".** A command telling the Israelites to listen to God.
v19 commandments. Instructions, rules. The "Ten Commandments" were given by God to show his rescued people how to live.	**v30 heart, soul, mind, strength.** Every part of you.
	Mark 10:13-16
v19 commit adultery. Have sex with a person who is married to someone else.	**v13 rebuked.** Strongly criticised, told off.
v19 give false testimony. Tell lies about someone.	**v14 indignant.** Angry.
	v14 hinder. Prevent, stop.
v19 defraud. Cheat someone to steal their money.	**v14 the kingdom of God.** God's kingdom is not a place. It is God's people living with him as their King now and for ever.
v19 honour. Respect.	
v21 lack. Do not have.	**v14 such as these.** People like these children.
v22 the man's face fell. He looked sad and unhappy.	**v15 receive.** Accept.
v22 wealth. Riches, a lot of money.	**v16 blessed them.** Prayed for them.

👁 **Re-read Mark 10:17-22**

1. What did the rich man want to know (see verse 17)?

He wanted to know what he needed to do to inherit eternal life.

2. What commandments did the man say he had kept (see verses 19-20)?

The man said that he had kept these commandments:

- do not murder
- do not commit adultery
- do not steal
- do not give false testimony
- do not defraud
- honour your father and mother.

These are the last six of the Ten Commandments that God gave to the Israelites (see Exodus 20:1-17 and Deuteronomy 5:6-21).

These are the commandments that describe how to love other people.

Note: The first four commandments are missing from the list Jesus gave the man.

The first four commandments describe the way we should treat God:

- have no other gods
- have no idols – don't worship or pray to pretend gods
- do not misuse God's name
- keep his Sabbath – the day he said his people should do no work.

Later in the session we will see that Jesus shows the man that he has not kept these first four commandments.

👁 Read aloud Mark 12:28-30

If your group members have English as a second language, encourage them to read the passage a second time in their own language.

Depending on your group, it may be appropriate to go through some or all of the Bible words listed on page 27 of the Handbook at this point. The word list for this study is also shown on page 56 of this Leader's Guide.

👁 Re-read Mark 12:28-30

Note: Verses 29-30 sum up the first four of the Ten Commandments. For your own interest, verse 31 (not read in this session) sums up the remaining six.

3. What did Jesus say was the most important commandment (see verses 29-30)?

Jesus said the most important commandment is to love God with all your heart, soul, mind and strength. That means to love God with every part of you.

This summarises the first four of the Ten Commandments (Exodus 20:1-11).

🔜 *Read the note printed on page 26 of the Handbook. It says:*

Jesus said we must love God with every part of our lives.

4. What did Jesus say the rich man should do (see Mark 10:21)? The man thought that he loved God. How did this show him that he did not love God with every part of his life (see Mark 10:22)?

Jesus told the man to sell everything he had and give his money away to the poor.

But the man "went away sad, because he had great wealth" (verse 22).

Jesus did this to show the man that he loved his money more than he loved God. Jesus is lovingly pointing the man to the truth. Jesus isn't setting a trap for the man – the loving thing to do is to break the man's trust in the things he has done, since these things can never earn eternal life.

Note: Jesus does not expect everyone to sell all their possessions and give their money away if they want to follow him. But he does expect us to love God more than anything else.

5. The man loved being rich more than he loved God. What other things do people love more than God?

This question is designed to help your group think about some of the things that we can treat as being more important than God, eg: family, money, education, career, reputation, looks and image, being accepted by friends, bringing honour to your family…

It will help group members apply what they have learned to their own lives.

🔜 *Read the note printed on page 27 of the Handbook. It says:*

None of us deserves eternal life because none of us has loved God as we should.

👁 **Read aloud Mark 10:13-16**

📖 If your group members have English as a second language, encourage them to read the passage a second time in their own language.

📖 Depending on your group, it may be appropriate to go through some or all of the Bible words listed on page 27 of the Handbook at this point. The word list for this study is also shown on page 92 of this Leader's Guide.

👁 **Re-read Mark 10:13-16**

Note: It's possible that someone may be concerned about Jesus "touching" the children (in the light of today's right concerns about child protection). If anyone asks, explain that it simply means Jesus placing his hands on a child – probably their head or shoulder – while praying for them. The parents were with their children at the time, and had brought them to Jesus so that he could place his hands on the children and bless them.

6. What did the children need to do in order to belong to the kingdom of God?

Nothing. They simply came to Jesus.

Note: Verse 14 says the kingdom of God "belongs to such as these". Verse 15 refers to those who "receive the kingdom of God". For those who are in God's kingdom it can be said both that they belong to it, and that it belongs to them.

7. How can anyone enter the kingdom of God (see verse 15)?

By receiving it like a little child.

Little children are entirely dependent on adults. In the same way, we are entirely dependent on God's goodness in offering us the free gift of forgiveness and eternal life.

Note: Jesus' phrase here does not mean children are innocent or pure – neither of these things are seen in most children!

You might want also to ask your group: **Who will never enter the kingdom of God?** The answer is anyone who will not receive it like a little child – anyone who depends on themselves (who they are, what they've done or not done) instead of depending entirely on God's goodness. Anyone who will not come empty-handed and completely dependent on God's grace cannot enter.

Don't worry that you have nothing to give God to enter his kingdom. But more than that, never think or hope you have something to give God to "earn" a place in his kingdom. You will never enter that way.

Read the note printed on page 27 of the Handbook. It says:

> **The only way to enter the kingdom of God is to come to Jesus like a little child.**
> **We cannot earn eternal life. It is a free gift for everyone who comes to Jesus and puts their trust in him. The Bible calls this grace.**

8. What is wrong with the man's question in Mark 10:17?

The problem with the man's question is that he believes he can *do* something to inherit eternal life. He cannot, because – like all of us – he is sinful.

But, rather than treating us as we deserve, God shows us amazing grace and generosity. He offers us forgiveness – forgiveness that is only made possible by Jesus' death on the cross.

We simply need to accept this gift from him. There's nothing we can do to earn it.

TO FINISH

Read the summary printed on page 28 of the Handbook. It says:

> **We are all like the man in Mark 10.**
> **We do not love God with every part of our lives.**
>
> **We deserve to be punished.**

> **But God the Father loves us so much that he sent his Son to rescue us.**
> **Jesus died to pay the price for our sin.**

> **We cannot earn God's forgiveness and eternal life by doing good things.**
> **God gives us the gift of forgiveness and eternal life if we put our trust in Jesus Christ.**
>
> **This is what grace is – a gift from God that we don't deserve and cannot earn.**
> **God will accept everyone who comes to Jesus and puts their trust in him.**

▣ *If you feel it is appropriate for your group, you may like to show episode 6 of the* Christianity Explored *DVD at this point. The DVD can be used as a summary or a refresher for the main teaching point of this session. However, it also includes Bible passages and concepts that have not been covered in this Bible study, so please watch it in advance to judge whether or not your group members would find it helpful.*

▣ *If it's appropriate for your group, ask them to read Mark 14:1 – 16:8 before the next session. There's space at the back of the group member's Handbook, on page 39, for them to write down any questions they have.*

▣ *Thank your group members for coming and encourage them to come back next time. Tell them:* We've seen that we cannot earn God's forgiveness and eternal life by doing good things. Forgiveness is an undeserved gift from God. He gives eternal life to everyone who puts their trust in Jesus. That's what a Christian is – someone who is trusting Jesus to give them eternal life rather than trusting in what they have done. Next time we will think about what it means to follow Jesus.

AFTERWARDS

▣ Did you manage to keep the focus on the big idea of this session? ie: that we cannot earn forgiveness by doing good things, but that it is a free gift from God for everyone who puts their trust in Jesus.

▣ Did any of the group members ask a question or make a comment that you could follow up? If so, plan how you will do that, as well as praying for that person.

▣ Thank God for each group member, and pray that God will open their hearts to the amazing truth of his grace and mercy.

▣ If you are going to give out copies of an evangelistic booklet or tract at the end of the next session, make sure you have enough copies. You can find a list of recommended booklets at **www.ceministries.org**.

▣ Alternatively, if you think an online presentation might suit your group better, have a look at the six-minute video on the *Christianity Explored* evangelistic website. This is based on Mark's Gospel and will reinforce many of the points covered in this course. You can find it at **www.christianityexplored.org/what-is-christianity**.

What does it mean to follow Jesus?

7

THE BIG IDEA

Following Jesus means "denying ourselves" – no longer living for ourselves, but for Jesus. We need to be prepared to "take up our cross" – to follow Jesus whatever the cost.

🔲 *Ask everyone to turn to Session 7 on page 29 of the Christianity Explored Universal Handbook.*

🔲 *If you suggested that your group read Mark 14:1 – 16:8 at home, ask if they have any questions about what they read. The appendix on page 125 lists common questions from Mark along with suggestions for answering them.*

🔲 *Read the summary of Session 6, called "The story so far", on page 29 of the Handbook. It says:*

- **Christianity is the good news (the "gospel") about Jesus Christ.**

- **Jesus is the Son of God. He has the power and authority of God himself.**

- **We have all sinned. We all face God's punishment. We all need to be forgiven.**

- **Jesus came to rescue us from hell, the punishment our sin deserves.**

- **God punished Jesus for our sin. Jesus died on a cross to pay the price for our sin.**

- **Jesus rose from the dead, just as he said he would.**

- **We cannot earn eternal life by doing good things.**

Leader's checklist

Have you...

- ☐ Reminded group members where and when you will meet (eg: by email or text message)?

- ☐ Prepared food and drinks?

- ☐ Enough Gospels, Bibles or printed-out sheets with the Bible passages on them?

- ☐ Handbooks for each person, plus spares if needed?

- ☐ Thought through your answers to each of the questions?

- ☐ Prayed for each group member and yourself as the leader?

- ☐ The optional Christianity Explored DVD ready to play?

- ☐ Evangelistic booklets or tracts to give to group members, or details of the video on the Christianity Explored website (see page 97).

- **God gives us the gift of forgiveness and eternal life if we put our trust in Jesus Christ.**

➡ *Explain that in this session we will find out what it means to follow Jesus.*

OPENING DISCUSSION QUESTION

➡ *Ask your group the following question.*

What do you think when you hear the word "Christian"?

You may want to write down the group's answers so that you can refer to them later.

BIBLE DISCUSSION

➡ *Ask the group members to turn to Mark 8 in their Gospels, Bibles or printed sheets.*

👁 Read aloud Mark 8:27-30

➡ *If your group members have English as a second language, encourage them to read the passage a second time in their own language. This will help them to understand the passage better. It will also help them if and when they return home – see page 33.*

➡ *There is a list of Bible words from this week's passages (NIV) on pages 30-31 of the group member's Handbook. Depending on your group, it may be appropriate to go through some or all of these words at this point. The word list for this study is also shown opposite.*

Bible words	
Mark 8:27-38	**v32 aside.** To one side.
v27 disciples. Jesus' twelve closest friends.	**v32 rebuke.** Criticise strongly.
	v33 Satan. The devil.
v27 Caesarea Philippi. A town in the north of Israel. See map on page 4.	**v33 the things of God.** What God says is good and important.
v28 John the Baptist. A prophet. John baptized people (by dipping them under water) to show that they wanted to be washed clean of their sins by God.	**v33 the things of men.** What people want, or think should be important.
	v34 come after me. Follow me.
	v34 deny himself. Not live for himself.
v28 Elijah. An important prophet from the Old Testament part of the Bible.	**v34 take up his cross.** Be ready to suffer (as Jesus suffered on the cross).
v28 prophets. Messengers from God.	**v35 the gospel.** The good news about Jesus.
v29 Christ. A Greek word that means "God's chosen King". The same word in the Hebrew language is "Messiah".	**v36 forfeit.** Lose.
	v36 soul. Spirit.
v31 the Son of Man. A title (name) Jesus often used about himself.	**v38 adulterous and sinful generation.** People who have turned away from God.
v31 elders, chief priests and teachers of the law. Three groups of Jewish religious leaders.	**v38 comes in his Father's glory with the holy angels.** Comes from heaven as God's chosen, glorious King.
v31 rise again. Come back to life.	
v32 plainly. Clearly.	

👁 **Re-read Mark 8:27-30**

1. What did Jesus ask his disciples in verse 27?

He asked them who people said he was.

2. In verse 28, who did most people say Jesus was?

- Some people said he was John the Baptist, who Mark mentions in chapters 1 and 6.

- Others said he was Elijah, perhaps the best known and most important prophet in Israel's history.

- Others said he was perhaps another prophet.

All of the people listed were dead, and all were important prophets – messengers from God.

3. Peter answered Jesus' question correctly. Who did he say Jesus is (see verse 29)?

Peter said that Jesus is the Christ. That means God's chosen King.

Note: The Greek word "Christ" and the Hebrew word "Messiah" both mean "the Anointed One". In the Old Testament, kings were anointed (by having oil poured on their head) to show that they had been chosen by God.

4. How would you answer the question Jesus asked in verse 29?

This question is designed to show what the group members understand and believe about Jesus.

👁 Read aloud Mark 8:31-33

If your group members have English as a second language, encourage them to read the passage a second time in their own language.

Depending on your group, it may be appropriate to go through some or all of the Bible words listed on pages 30-31 of the Handbook at this point. The word list for this study is also shown on page 65 of this Leader's Guide.

👁 Re-read Mark 8:31-33

Read the note printed on page 30 of the Handbook. It says:

"Christ" is a title. It means "God's chosen King". Jesus is the King who came to bring people into God's kingdom.

5. The people of Israel were expecting the Christ to come and save them from their enemies. What did Jesus say he had come to do (see verse 31)?

Jesus said he had come to suffer, to be rejected by Israel's religious leaders and be killed. He promised that he would rise from the dead three days later.

6. How did Peter react to what Jesus said (see verse 32)?

Peter took Jesus to one side and started to rebuke him. Peter could not accept that what Jesus said was true.

7. Why did Peter react like this (see verse 33)?

Peter had in mind the things of men, not the things of God.

Peter was thinking from a human point of view. The people were expecting that God's chosen King – the Christ – would save them from their enemies. So Peter was probably hoping that Jesus had come to save them from the Romans.

Peter could not accept that Jesus must suffer and die. He did not understand that this was how the Christ would be their Saviour and King.

Peter understood *who* Jesus was – but he did not understand *why* Jesus came.

Note: Peter didn't want Jesus to suffer and die because that wouldn't serve "the things of men". But Peter wasn't the only one who didn't want Jesus to die in this way. Jesus understood that Satan didn't want him to fulfil "the things of God" either. In trying to stop Jesus from going through suffering, rejection and death, Peter was working with Satan, not with God. This is why Jesus says: "Get behind me, Satan!"

Read the note printed on page 31 of the Handbook. It says:

God the Father had a plan for his Son, Jesus Christ.
God's plan was very different from what Peter expected.

8. Think about what you have already learned from Mark's Gospel. Why did Jesus have to be killed and rise again?

Jesus had to suffer and die to save us from our greatest problem, God's judgment on our sin.

Jesus died to rescue us from hell, the punishment our sin deserves.

Jesus did not come to be served as a king, but to serve us by dying for us. He gave his life as the ransom to free us from our sin (Mark 10:45).

👁 **Read aloud Mark 8:34-38**

💬 *If your group members have English as a second language, encourage them to read the passage a second time in their own language.*

💬 *Depending on your group, it may be appropriate to go through some or all of the Bible words listed on page 31 of the Handbook at this point. The word list for this study is also shown on page 65 of this Leader's Guide.*

👁 **Re-read Mark 8:34-38**

9. What did Jesus say that following him would mean (see verse 34)?

We must deny ourselves and take up our cross.

💬 *Ask your group what they think these two phrases mean.*

• To "deny ourselves" means living for Jesus instead of living for ourselves. We must turn away from our self-centredness and self-reliance. We cannot follow Jesus unless we deny our own selfish instincts.

• To "take up our cross" means we must be prepared to serve Jesus – and others – to the point of giving up our lives. Jesus must be more important to us than life itself.

Note: Look at what happened immediately before Jesus says this (verses 31-33). Jesus was talking about why he came – about the cross. Then Jesus immediately turned his attention from the cross *he* must take up, to the cross *we* must take up.

It is costly to follow Jesus and will sometimes be painful for us.

10. Why is it wise to follow Jesus (see verses 35-38)?

Jesus gives us four reasons to follow him:

• If we give up our life for Jesus, we'll save it – and if we don't, we'll lose it (verse 35).

- We might "gain the whole world" (everything that matters to us) if we reject Jesus. But we still lose the most important thing we have – our soul (verse 36).

- If we miss out on eternal life, there's nothing we can do to buy it back (verse 37).

- If we follow Jesus, he will welcome us and not be ashamed of us when he comes from heaven as God's chosen, glorious King. But if we reject Jesus, then he will reject us (verse 38).

11. In what ways would you have to deny yourself to follow Jesus?

This question is designed to help group members think carefully about what following Jesus would mean for them personally.

Encourage them to think about how this would affect every part of their lives, eg: their relationships, what they spend their money on, how they use their time, what their priorities are for now and the future etc.

12. From what you have learned in Mark 8, describe what a Christian is. Use your own words.

This question is designed to help group members think carefully about what they have learned. They may phrase their answers in a variety of ways but you will want to ensure that they include both what they believe (eg: Mark 8:29, 31) and what this means for them (eg: Mark 8:34).

Their answers may show an area they are struggling to understand, in which case you will need to explain it again.

13. Would you use the words above to describe yourself?

This question is designed to reveal where group members are in their relationship with Christ. Use your judgement in deciding whether to ask them to explain their answers, but bear in mind that there will be opportunities to think further about their responses in the closing session.

TO FINISH

Read the summary printed on page 32 of the Handbook.

Jesus is the Christ – God's chosen King.

Jesus came to die – to pay the price for our sin.
He rose from the dead – just as he said he would.

Following Jesus means "denying ourselves" – no longer living for ourselves but for Jesus.
"Taking up our cross" means being prepared to follow Jesus, whatever the cost.

CH 10 - COM6 & DIE 17 MINS

- *If you feel it is appropriate for your group, you may like to show episode 7 of the* Christianity Explored *DVD at this point. The DVD can be used as a summary or a refresher for the main teaching point of this session. However, it also includes Bible passages and concepts that have not been covered in this Bible study, so please watch it in advance to judge whether or not your group members would find it helpful.*

- *If it's appropriate for your group, give them a copy of an evangelistic booklet to read, or ask them to watch an online video (see page 61).*

- *Thank your group members for coming and encourage them to come back for the final session. Tell them:* We've seen that following Jesus is the way we receive forgiveness and eternal life. It will affect every area of our lives. It means "denying ourselves" – living for Jesus instead of living for ourselves. And it means "taking up our cross" – following Jesus, whatever the cost. Next week we will bring together everything we have discovered from Mark's Gospel. We will look at a story Jesus told about how people respond to the good news about him, and think about what that means for us.

AFTERWARDS

- Did you manage to keep the focus on the big idea of this session? ie: that following Jesus means denying ourselves and taking up our cross.

- Did any of the group members ask a question or make a comment that you could follow up? If so, plan how you will do that, as well as praying for that person.

- Since the next session is the final one, think about what you could suggest that group members do next. See page 39 for suggestions.

- Thank God for each group member, and pray that they will respond to the call to follow Jesus.

What next?

8

THE BIG IDEA

The parable of the sower shows four different responses to the good news about Jesus:

1. hearing the word but quickly forgetting what they've heard

2. responding well at first but when trouble comes as a result of following Jesus, they stop following him

3. worries, money and other desires become more important than following Jesus

4. hearing the good news, accepting it and continuing to be changed by it.

Ask everyone to turn to Session 8 on page 33 of the Christianity Explored Universal Handbook.

If you suggested that your group read an evangelistic tract or watch a gospel video at home, ask if they have any questions about what they read or watched.

Read the summary of Session 7, called "The story so far", on page 33 of the Handbook. It says:

- **Christianity is the good news (the "gospel") about Jesus Christ, the Son of God.**

- **We have all sinned. We all face God's punishment. We all need to be forgiven.**

- **Jesus came to rescue us from hell, the punishment our sin deserves.**

- **God punished Jesus for our sin. Jesus died on a cross to pay the price for our sin.**

Leader's checklist

Have you...

☐ Reminded group members where and when you will meet (eg: by email or text message)?

☐ Prepared food and drinks?

☐ Enough Gospels, Bibles or printed-out sheets with the Bible passages on them?

☐ Handbooks for each person, plus spares if needed?

☐ Thought through your answers to each of the questions?

☐ Prayed for each group member and yourself as the leader?

☐ The optional Christianity Explored DVD ready to play?

☐ Information about what group members might do next. (See page 39 for suggestions.)

107

- **Jesus rose from the dead, just as he said he would.**

- **We cannot earn eternal life by doing good things.**

- **God gives us the gift of forgiveness and eternal life if we put our trust in Jesus Christ.**

- **Following Jesus means "denying ourselves" and "taking up our cross".**

Explain that in this session we will look at a story Jesus told about how people respond to him.

OPENING DISCUSSION QUESTION

Read aloud "The story so far" from the right-hand side of page 33 of the handbook. Then ask your group the following question.

Is there anything you do not understand?

You may find it helpful to use the summaries at the end of each session to help answer any questions the group ask. For example, if they don't understand the final point in "The story so far", which is about "denying ourselves" and "taking up our cross", then look back at the summary on page 32 of the Handbook, where these two phrases are explained.

BIBLE DISCUSSION

Ask the group members to turn to Mark 4 in their Gospels, Bibles or printed sheets.

Read aloud Mark 4:1-9 and 4:13-20

If your group members have English as a second language, encourage them to read the passage a second time in their own language. This will help them to understand the passage better. It will also help them if and when they return home – see page 33.

There is a list of Bible words from this week's passage (NIV) on pages 34-35 of the group member's Handbook. Depending on your group, it may be appropriate to go through some or all of these words at this point. The word list for this study is also shown opposite.

Bible words	
Mark 4:1-9	**Mark 4:13-20**
v1 gathered. Came together.	**v14 the word.** God's word, the good news about Jesus.
v1 shore. Beach, side of the lake.	**v15 sown.** Planted.
v2 parables. Stories with a deeper meaning.	**v15 Satan.** The devil.
v3 sow. Spread seed, plant.	**v16 receive.** Take, accept.
v4 scattering. Throwing, spreading.	**v17 root.** The part of a plant that grows into the soil to collect water.
v5 sprang up. Grew.	**v17 persecution.** Opposition. Being treated badly because of Jesus.
v5 shallow. Not deep.	**v17 fall away.** Stop following Jesus.
v6 scorched. Burned.	**v19 the deceitfulness of wealth.** The false promises of money.
v6 withered. Became weak and small.	**v19 desires.** Wishes, longings.
v7 choked. Strangled.	**v19 making it unfruitful.** Stopping it from growing fruit/grain.
v7 bear grain. Grow ears of grain.	
v8 crop. Harvest.	

Read the note printed on page 33 of the Handbook. It says:

Jesus often taught people by telling parables. A parable is a story with a deeper, sometimes hidden, meaning. In verses 3-8 Jesus tells the story. In verses 13-20 he explains what it means.

Re-read Mark 4:1-9 and 13-20

1. What is the "seed" in this parable? (See verses 3 and 14.)

The word of God – the Bible's message about Jesus.

2. What happens when people hear God's word in verses 4 and 15?

Satan (another name for the devil) comes and takes the word away.

Satan is God's enemy. He doesn't want people to hear the good news about Jesus so he will do what he can to make them ignore or forget it.

Read the note printed on page 34 of the Handbook. It says:

The path is like people who hear the good news about Jesus, but "Satan comes and takes away the word" (Mark 4:15).

They hear about Jesus but quickly forget what they have heard.

3. What happens when people hear God's word in verses 5-6 and 16-17?

People receive the word with joy but it has no root. When trouble comes because of following Jesus, the hearer gives up.

4. What does it mean that this kind of person who hears God's word "has no root"?

They don't understand that following Jesus mean "denying ourselves" and "taking up our cross" to follow him. (See Mark 8:34.) As a result, trouble or opposition will make them give up.

Read the note printed on page 34 of the Handbook. It says:

The rocky soil is like those who are happy about what they hear, but "they last only a short time" (Mark 4:16-17).

When trouble comes as a result of following Jesus, they stop following him.

5. What happens when people hear God's word in verses 7 and 18-19?

Worries, money and the desire for other things choke (strangle) the word.

6. How do worries, money and other desires choke God's word?

If we spend our time and energy on these things, we can't be spending them on following Jesus.

A lot of worries seem natural. But if we just focus on the things we are worried about, rather than turning to God to give us the good things we need, it will stop us trusting in the good news about Jesus.

A lot of people believe the lie that money will give them everything they want. But plenty of rich people live lonely, empty lives. This is the "deceitfulness of wealth" – the lie that money can give us what only God can give us: a right relationship with him, a loving Christian family and a certain future.

Nothing and no one is more important than Jesus. If we make worries, love of money and other desires more important than Jesus, it will stop us from following him.

🔲 *Read the note printed on page 35 of the Handbook. It says:*

> **The thorns are worries, money and the desires for other things. These things can seem more important than following Jesus.**

7. What happens when people hear God's word in verses 8 and 20?

People hear the word and accept it, and it continues to change them.

🔲 *Read the note printed on page 35 of the Handbook. It says:*

> **Those who are like good soil hear the good news about Jesus, accept it and continue to be changed by it.**

8. Which type of soil would you say best describes you? Why?

This question is designed to help group members think about their own response to the good news about Jesus.

Ask them to circle the picture that best describes them. They may also like to write something about their answer in the space below the pictures.

Optional question: Do you have any comments or questions?

If appropriate and you have time, you may want to ask if anyone has any comments or questions. This is the last opportunity for people to ask questions as part of a group. You may also want to offer them the opportunity to talk with you or another leader afterwards if they prefer.

CH7 THE Sower @ 13 mins

■ *If you feel it is appropriate for your group, you may like to show "The Sower" (Day Away part 1) of the* Christianity Explored *DVD at this point. The DVD can be used as a summary or a refresher for the main teaching point of this session. However, it also includes Bible passages and concepts that have not been covered in this Bible study, so please watch it in advance to judge whether or not your group members would find it helpful.*

■ *Read the note printed on page 36 of the Handbook.*

Jesus was clear about the right way to respond to God's word. "The time has come," he said. "The kingdom of God is near. Repent and believe the good news!" (Mark 1:15)

That means we must turn from what we know is wrong and trust in what Jesus has done for us when he died on the cross.

■ *Ask your group:*

How will you respond?

■ *Give the group an opportunity to respond. Understandably, some may not want to talk openly so offer to speak privately with people if they'd prefer.*

There are, broadly speaking, three possible responses group members could make at the end of the course:

For those who are not ready to follow Jesus, but would still like to learn more, you might suggest: coming to church with you, meeting with you for one-to-one Bible study, doing *Christianity Explored* again, or reading a good Christian book that addresses questions they may have. See "After the course" on page 39 for help in following up group members. You can find suggestions for recommended books from www.ceministries.org

For those who do not want to follow Jesus, and show no interest in taking things further: let them know how much you've enjoyed getting to know them, and offer to meet up for a coffee and a chat in a few weeks' time if they'd like.

For those who have heard the call to "repent and believe", and want to begin following Jesus: help them to understand what it means to "repent and believe". You could ask: "What do you think you need to do in order to begin following Jesus?" Let their answer guide your discussion. For example, if they say they need to say sorry to God and change how they live, ask them what that will mean for them personally. Help them to be clear about the need both to repent *and* to believe.

When you have talked about what it would mean for them personally to repent and believe, ask what they want to do now. Some may say they want to go away and think some more (and maybe re-read the evangelistic booklet they were given last session). Or they may want an opportunity to talk about this again at another time, in which case arrange a time to meet.

Some may want to begin following Jesus. If so, ask them to think about what they would like to say to God. They may struggle to know how to do this, in which case a simple way to pray is:

• **Sorry.** What do they need to say sorry for and turn away from? (ie: repent)

• **Thank you.** What do they believe God has done for them and want to thank him for?

• **Please.** What do they need God's help to do?

Encourage the group member(s) to use their own words to talk to God.

Note: Up to this point we have not included any prayer in *Christianity Explored*, so the group member(s) may not be sure what prayer is. Explain that praying is very simple. It is us talking to God and trusting that he hears us and will answer our prayer in the way he knows is best. Assure them that there's no need to use special words, we can just speak as we normally would. Some people like to finish a prayer by saying "Amen". This simply means "So be it" or "We agree".

After the group member has prayed, assure them that Jesus welcomes everyone who comes to him. Tell them that you will be praying for them as they continue to follow Jesus. If they don't already do so, encourage them to start coming regularly to church, and suggest a way that they can meet with other Christians so that they can help each other to live for Jesus.

In the New Testament, repentance and belief is always linked with baptism. This is a picture of being washed clean of our sin and starting a new life with God. It is also a public sign that someone is a Christian. So encourage any new believers to speak to their pastor or minister about being baptized.

Note: It may be your instinct to pray a "prayer of commitment" with someone who seems to be ready to follow Jesus. We have not included a prayer like this in *Christianity Explored* for a good reason. **Becoming a Christian is not about a formula of saying some magic words.** It is about God working in you by his Spirit to bring about genuine repentance and faith in Christ. It is true that prayers like this can genuinely help some people express to God their desire to turn to Christ. But they can also give false assurance to others, who believe they must be genuine believers because they have "prayed the prayer".

In addition, guiding and helping people towards saying their own prayer to God will make it more genuine, heartfelt and real for them. They will be saying to God what they know and feel, and want to do for themselves.

Of course, as course leader, you have the freedom to point your group to a particular prayer. But we urge you to think carefully about the possible negative effects of using a form of prayer, and the advantages of encouraging a more individual response to the gospel they have heard.

As this is the end of the course, let the group know about the things they could do next (eg: discipleship courses or future Christianity Explored courses). Since they have just read through one book of the Bible, you might want to suggest that they pick one of the remaining 65 and read through that. It may be useful to have Bible-reading notes available to help anyone who wants to begin reading the Bible for themself. Notes in many languages and in simple English are available online. You (and any other leaders) might also want to share with the group how and when you do your own personal reading of the Bible.

As you are saying goodbye to the group, however they have responded, let them know how much you've enjoyed having them on the course. And do continue to pray for all your group members once the course has ended.

AFTERWARDS

- Did you manage to keep the focus on the big idea of this session? ie: the four different responses to following Jesus and the need for each of us to consider how we will respond to him.

- Did any of the group members ask to meet individually with a leader or to join another course or group? If so, plan how you will arrange that, as well as praying for that person.

- Thank God for each group member. Pray for each one according to the response they have made. Ask God to help and encourage any who have started to follow Jesus, and to open the hearts of those who are undecided or who show no interest in exploring Christianity further.

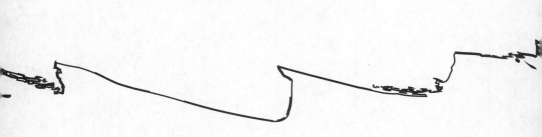

Answering tough questions

OPEN TO QUESTION

One of the most important aspects of running a course like *Christianity Explored Universal* is that it encourages guests to ask questions in an environment where they will be taken seriously, and not be ridiculed or belittled. You should encourage your group with words like: "No question is too simple, or too difficult – *Christianity Explored* is about you finding answers to the important questions of life".

It is this atmosphere of open enquiry that encourages people to "open up" about spiritual things, and to approach the Bible not as a dead textbook, but as the source for answers. It is your job to help create this environment by your openness, honesty and willingness to talk in a relaxed way about things that group members may find particularly difficult to articulate.

WHY PEOPLE DON'T ASK QUESTIONS

There are a number of reasons why people won't ask questions:

- **Because they don't have any!** Some guests may not have thought much about spiritual things. It may be they grew up in a Christian home, and didn't question the things they have always been taught. However, the word of God often provokes reactions and questions. So in the course of reading Mark, they are likely to come up with some. And if they are part of a larger group that is dealing with questions, then they will be encouraged to join in. Don't force the issue – let them develop in their own time.

- **Because they are frightened of appearing stupid.** This is a BIG issue for many people. If they think the question is simple, or that they will be made fun of by others for asking it, then they will not speak up. The key here is to make sure you keep repeating the words: "No question is too simple, or too difficult – *Christianity Explored* is about you finding answers to the important questions of life".

- **Because they are shy.** Some people simply aren't good at speaking up in groups. And that is fine. Just make sure that you are able to talk with them personally about their questions. Watch out for the tell-tale signs of a wrinkled forehead as they read or listen.

- **Because they need time.** Some people just need more time to get to the question. They may think of something later that evening or during the next week. So you should always give an opportunity to deal with questions from the previous session that have occurred to people, and don't make them feel that everyone is taking a step backwards because "all that was dealt with last time".

WHY DO PEOPLE ASK QUESTIONS?

It might seem obvious: "Because they want to know the answer" – but it often runs much deeper than that:

- **Because I want to test you.** The precise question they ask may not be of particular concern to them. It could just be that they have heard it expressed by others, or know that it is a tricky question for Christians to answer. What they are more interested in is how you handle it (*see page 121*). By not being rattled, and by taking the question seriously and demonstrating that you have given it some thought, you are answering "the question behind the question", which is: are these people trustworthy? Always take questions seriously.

- **Because I genuinely don't understand.** There may be a huge variation in Bible knowledge in your group, and some will want to ask what you might consider to be really basic questions: "Who was Jesus?", "When did all this happen?", "What is prayer?" etc. Again, treat them seriously, and make sure the rest of the group do not look down on those with less knowledge than they have.

- **Because I have had a distressing personal experience.** There is a world of difference between someone asking: "Why does God allow suffering?" as an academic question, and someone who asks the same question having watched a close relative die of cancer recently. The way you answer the two may be completely different. And of course, you will not know if others listening in to your answer are carrying a burden of disappointment or personal pain. Always answer compassionately.

- **Because I have been let down.** The way a question is phrased may be the key to getting an insight here. So instead of "What is prayer?", asking "Why does God answer some prayers and not others?" may indicate that the questioner has some specific disappointment in mind. Similarly, a question about Christians being hypocrites may relate to some bitter personal experience of a Christian or a church in the past. Always answer honestly.

▪ **Because I want to be sure it all makes sense.** The interest in a particular question may not be because it is a problem, but rather that they are seeking a sense that the Christian faith as a whole sticks together coherently. So answering in a way that connects the question with the big picture of the Bible's message is important. Answer from the Bible, not just from sensible reasons or philosophy.

HOW DO I ANSWER?

The following two appendices give you some suggested approaches to answering the substance of the difficult questions that people ask. But, as we have suggested above, it is equally important that we answer in the right way. 1 Peter 3:15-16 says:

> "But in your hearts set apart Christ as Lord[1]. Always be prepared[2] to give an answer to everyone who asks you to give the reason[3] for the hope that you have. But do this with gentleness and respect.[4]"

Notice four things about giving answers:

1. **The person who answers the questions needs to be someone who is personally committed to the lordship of Christ.** This is important, because the answer to their unspoken questions is not your arguments or knowledge – it is your life. Many of their most important questions will remain unarticulated, like: "Is this relevant to me?", "What does this look like in a real person?" and "Could I be a Christian?" All these questions are answered by the way you live and model being a disciple and follower of Jesus. Are you displaying the joy, peace, love and contentment in life that comes from knowing Christ as Lord? If you come to a session feeling resentful, angry and doubtful in your own standing with God, then you cannot hope to influence your group members for the gospel. They may hear convincing arguments from your mouth, but your life will speak much more loudly.

2. **You must be ready to answer.** Take time to think through the answers on the following pages, and come to your own conclusions about them. You should be as sure in your answer as the Bible is – no less, no more! For example, on the questions of the origin of evil, or the reason for suffering, we do not have final

and complete answers from the Bible, and therefore, we must be careful in what we say and acknowledge our difficulty with these issues, rather than insisting that we have it all sewn up.

3. **You must have a reasonable answer.** In other words, saying: "Just have faith in the Bible" is not enough – even if we cannot prove it with complete certainty, we have to show the reasonableness of our faith.

4. **You must answer gently and respectfully.** Even (perhaps especially) when people are hostile, we must model kindness, love and fairness in our attitudes, thinking and speaking. Only in this way will we win people for the gospel.

MORE TIPS ON ANSWERING QUESTIONS

Involve the group. Resist the temptation to answer the question on your own. It is good practice to first ask: "Does anyone else find this a difficult question?" You can then address your answers to the whole group. It may also be that you have Christians in your group who will be able to help answer. So you might ask: "Has anyone in the group got an answer to that?" In this way you are also training and encouraging the Christians to get involved in the discussion. It has been the experience on many *Christianity Explored* courses that involving the group in answering questions often helps other "not-yet-Christians" start to see the wrong thinking in some of their doubts as they start to argue back with a questioner!

Go to the Bible. The Bible is the sword of the Spirit, so we must have confidence that if we direct people to its answers, God will do his work through it. If you can, go to a Bible passage to read and then explain, especially if it is in Mark's Gospel.

Empathize. Don't give the impression that you have everything figured out. If you have wrestled with this question in the past – tell them. If you still have areas that you wrestle with, say so, but also tell them why it is no longer a problem in the larger scheme of your faith. For example: "I find suffering (eg: a natural disaster such as a major earthquake) very difficult to understand, but I know that God weeps over it too and cares, because he sent Jesus into the world, and he has experienced the pain and suffering of our broken world."

■ **Give them time.** Don't assume that they will sort out everything right at that moment. Many of the ideas and arguments and thoughts from the Bible will take time to sink in and be processed. Leave the question open for another day, and encourage them to think about it seriously over the next week, eg: "There are some big things to think about there, and you might not feel this discussion has answered all your questions immediately, but can I ask you to think about it, and maybe we can return to it next time if you want to go into it in more depth."

And finally...

Don't be afraid to admit that you don't know the answer to a question. But do promise to find out before the next session.

You will find help in answering questions in the next two appendices (starting on pages 125 and 133). In addition, **www.christianityexplored.org** includes video clips giving answers to popular questions.

Two *Christianity Explored* websites to help you:

www.christianityexplored.org
For non-Christians whether or not they're on a course

www.ceministries.org
For leaders looking for information, downloads and resources

Questions from Mark's Gospel

MARK 1:2-3

What are these strange quotes at the start?

Mark quotes from the Jewish Bible (what we call the Old Testament) – Malachi 3:1 and Isaiah 40:3 (written 600 years before Jesus was born). They are quotes from passages that promise a messenger who will announce the arrival of a rescuer King – the Christ or Messiah, who will save God's people from judgment. The promise of a messenger is clearly fulfilled by John the Baptist in Mark 1:4-8. Even his clothing (Mark 1:6) was like that of an Old Testament prophet, in particular Elijah (2 Kings 1:8).

MARK 1:13

What are angels?

The word literally means "messenger". They are spiritual beings in the service of God, who particularly are sent to deliver messages. An angel delivers the wonderful message of the resurrection in Mark 16:5-6. He is described as looking like a young man dressed in a white robe. No mention of wings!

MARK 1:23-27

What are evil spirits and demons?

The Bible says that there is an unseen spiritual world, which includes angels and evil spirits. According to the Bible, Satan, or the devil, is a fallen angel who is in rebellion against God and hostile to God's people. Demons are part of that fallen spiritual world, and serve Satan. Although Satan and his demons are powerful, the New Testament shows that Jesus has overcome Satan by the power of his death on the cross (see Colossians 2:15).

Note: If this topic comes up, deal with it briefly but don't allow it to dominate the session – some people are fascinated by "the dark side" and want to talk about it for hours. And make sure you explain to them that Christians have nothing to fear from the devil – Jesus has defeated him.

MARK 1:34; 7:36

Why did Jesus tell the people he healed not to tell anyone?

No one has ever healed people as Jesus did. It was instantaneous, spectacular and complete. People didn't just "start to feel a bit better". They were completely better immediately. Not surprisingly Jesus drew huge crowds who wanted to see these amazing miracles, but who seemed less interested in his teaching. Jesus did not want people coming just to see signs and wonders. He rejected such people (Mark 8:11-13). In Mark 1:45 it becomes clear that he has to leave the crowds in order to teach. He probably told people not to tell anyone so that the crowds would not become a problem.

MARK 2:10

Why did Jesus call himself the Son of Man?

"Son of man" is a Jewish term meaning simply "a man". But "Son of Man" is also a well-known title used in the Old Testament for the Messiah – God's promised King. See Daniel 7:13-14. The religious leaders would have understood that when Jesus used the title "Son of Man", it was a claim to be the Messiah.

MARK 2:16

What is a Pharisee?

This group of strict Jews did not just obey the Old Testament but held to many strict traditions. They were seen as some of the most holy men in Israel. But Jesus called them "hypocrites", which literally means "play-actors", because of the way they showed off their religion and self-righteousness. He strongly condemns them in passages such as Mark 7:6-9.

MARK 2:19

Who is the "bridegroom"?

Jesus is making the point that, for the disciples, fasting (going without food) is totally inappropriate when he's with them, just as it would be for wedding guests to be miserable at a wedding. Jesus is saying he is the bridegroom of God's people. This is another claim to be the Messiah promised in the Old Testament (Isaiah 54:5; 62:4-5; Hosea 2:16-20).

MARK 2:21-22

What is the new cloth/old coat, new wine/old skins story about?

People complained that Jesus was not following the religious rules of his day (Mark 2:18). Jesus says that the faith he has come to bring is not about rules at all. Jesus cannot be "fitted into" their "religion of rules". He came to bring a living friendship with God, not rules. Jesus brings grace, love and peace – not religious rules.

MARK 2:23

What is the Sabbath?

The Sabbath was the special day of rest when no work was done. The Sabbath was an opportunity for God's people to remember God's creation and how he rescued them from Egypt.

MARK 3:6

Who are the Herodians?

These were supporters of Herod Antipas, the king of Judea, who depended on the controlling Roman Empire for his power. They would have seen Jesus as a threat to Herod's rule.

MARK 3:13-19

Why did Jesus choose twelve apostles?

Jesus calls the twelve apostles on a mountainside. In the Old Testament God shows himself to his people on mountains (eg: Genesis 8; Exodus 19; and 1 Kings 18). There were twelve tribes of Israel – God's people in the Old Testament. Jesus is making the point that God is calling a new group of people to follow him.

MARK 3:22

What does it mean to be possessed by Beelzebub?

Beelzebub is another name for the devil. Note that the religious authorities don't question whether Jesus is powerful or whether the miracles happen. They simply ask where his power comes from. They say that Jesus is possessed by the devil and is driving out demons. Jesus replies that their claim is foolish – after all, if the "prince of demons" really was driving out other demons, then he would be fighting against himself.

MARK 3:29

What is the blasphemy against the Holy Spirit that will never be forgiven?

The religious leaders have seen Jesus perform wonderful miracles, and have heard his astonishing teaching. Now they claim that the work of the Holy Spirit is actually the work of the devil. Jesus' warning has nothing to do with swearing at the Holy Spirit – in simple terms, it means rejecting the only way of forgiveness that God has provided. Of course, this sin is only unforgivable for as long as a person goes on committing it. Many of the same religious leaders changed their minds about Jesus later, and so were forgiven (Acts 6:7). This is vital to understand. There can be no forgiveness if we reject Jesus.

MARK 4:2

Why did Jesus teach in parables?

Jesus told these memorable stories to teach spiritual truths. Parables have a clear surface meaning, but also a deeper meaning (often just one main point), which Jesus explains to those who will listen (Mark 4:1-34). There is a spiritual principle here: "To everyone who has, more will be given" (Luke 19:26). The disciples are intrigued by the parables and draw nearer to Jesus to hear the explanation. But, to the crowd, the parables are just curious stories. They hear, but do not understand (Mark 4:12). All people are like moths or bats reacting to light. They are either attracted to Jesus' teaching, or repelled by it.

MARK 4:40

Why does Jesus say: "Do you still have no faith?"

Despite all the evidence they've seen, the disciples still don't have faith in Jesus (note: to "have faith" in someone means to trust him or her). The disciples express terror rather than trust both before and after Jesus acts. Interestingly, just before this miracle, Jesus has told three parables making the point that God's word is powerful. He then calms the storm with a word. The disciples should have drawn the obvious conclusion.

MARK 6:3

Did Jesus have brothers and sisters?

These were the natural children of Joseph and Mary, conceived after the birth of Jesus. See also Mark 3:32. This answers the question as to whether Mary remained a virgin after the birth of Jesus. In addition, Matthew 1:25 certainly implies that Joseph and Mary had a normal sexual relationship after Jesus was born.

MARK 6:7-11

Why did Jesus send out the twelve disciples?

Jesus sends out the twelve disciples, telling them to expect some to accept and some to reject their message. They are to reject those who, by refusing to listen, reject them. The reference to shaking off dust refers to what Jews did on returning to Israel from Gentile countries, which they viewed as "unclean". For the disciples to do it in a Jewish village was like calling the village Gentile! It is a mark of judgment (see also Acts 13:51).

MARK 6:14-29

Why is there all this stuff about John the Baptist?

Mark tells us about the death of John the Baptist to make an important point. It answers the question that is implied in Mark 6:1-13: why don't people see who Jesus is? The answer is that people reject Jesus because, like Herod, they will not repent. In other words, they will not turn from their rebellion against God.

MARK 7:24-30

Why does Jesus call this woman a dog?

Mark tells us this incident to show that Jesus has come to rescue and save Gentiles as well as Jews. The woman is a Gentile (= non Jew) from near the city of Tyre. "Children" here refers to the Jews, and "dogs" was a common, unflattering expression that Jews used for any Gentile person. So Jesus is saying: "It isn't right to take what belongs to the Jews and give it to you Gentiles." In her reply (v 28) the woman is saying; "Yes Lord – I acknowledge that as a Gentile woman I have no right to ask help from you, the Jewish Messiah. But you have such great power and mercy that you must have enough to help me as well!" Jesus is impressed by her faith and her persistence, and grants her request.

MARK 8:15

What is the yeast of the Pharisees and Herod?

Yeast – the stuff you put in bread to make it rise – is used as a picture in the New Testament to refer to the influence of someone or something. Just as a tiny amount of yeast has a great effect on the whole batch of dough, so Jesus warns against being affected by the sinful attitudes of the Pharisees and Herod: specifically, these would be hypocrisy and worldliness.

MARK 8:17-21

Why do the disciples not understand?

Jesus has fed thousands in the desert (twice), healed people, forgiven sin, cast out evil spirits and stilled storms with a word. So what's wrong with the disciples? As the following two stories show – they need spiritual help to understand the truth that is staring them in the face. Spiritual truth can only be revealed by God's Spirit.

MARK 8:22-25

Why is there a two-part healing?

Jesus hasn't lost his touch, or found it difficult to heal this man. He is doing the healing as a kind of "acted parable", to explain what happens next. When Peter announces that Jesus is "the Christ" in Mark 8:29, he is like the man in Mark 8:24 (he has partial sight). It is clear from the verses that follow – where Peter rebukes Jesus – that although he has understood *who* Jesus is, he has not yet realized *why* Jesus has come (Mark 8:30-33).

MARK 8:32-33

Why does Jesus say: "Get behind me Satan!"?

Peter had recognized that Jesus was the Christ, but he could not understand why Jesus had to suffer and die. Jesus recognizes in Peter's words a temptation to reject God's plan that the Christ should die on the cross. It is not that Peter is Satan, or that Satan has "taken control". It is just that Peter is saying what the devil wants, which is to knock Jesus off course in his mission to rescue us by dying on the cross and rising to life again.

MARK 9:1

What does Jesus mean when he says that some "will not taste death before they see the kingdom of God come with power"?

This probably refers to the transfiguration of Jesus, recorded immediately after (Mark 9:2-7), although it could also be a reference to the coming of the Holy Spirit on the Day of Pentecost (Acts 1:8).

MARK 9:4

Who are Elijah and Moses?

Both of these people represent the Old Testament: Moses was the law-giver and Elijah the greatest of the Old Testament prophets. The fact that they talk with Jesus shows that he is the one the Old Testament is pointing to.

MARK 9:11-13

What does Jesus mean when he says: "Elijah does come first"?

The disciples have failed to recognize that John the Baptist was the Elijah-like messenger promised in Malachi 4:5-6 who would come before "the Lord". Elijah

was a prophet in the eighth century BC who lived out in the wilderness, wearing animal skins and a leather belt (2 Kings 1:8). This is how John the Baptist is described in Mark 1:6. Jesus makes it clear that John was the fulfilment of the prophecy concerning Elijah.

MARK 9:43-48

Why does Jesus tell us to cut our hands off?

Jesus obviously did not intend that a Christian should physically cut off a hand or foot, or pluck out an eye. It's not as if sin is confined to a particular part of our bodies. Jesus is exaggerating to make a point: "If anything is stopping you from entering the kingdom of God, it is better to take drastic action to rid yourself of it, whatever it is, than to end up in hell for ever." The most important thing is getting right with God. The logic is obvious: temporary pain is better than eternal punishment.

MARK 10:1-12

What does Jesus think about divorce?

Jesus makes it clear that divorce is always against the perfect purpose of God. God's plan in creation is that married people should live together for their whole lives (see Genesis 2:24). Jesus says that if people seek a divorce because they have found an alternative partner, such action is adultery (Mark 10:11-12). It is only because people's hearts are so hard (Mark 10:5) that divorce could ever be permitted. The danger is either that we use the concession of verse 5 as an excuse for deliberate sin, or that we think that divorce cuts us off from God for ever. Christ came to die for all sin, including the failures of divorce.

Note: Be aware that you are likely to have people in your group who have experienced the reality of broken marriages. For some this may be a significant personal issue.

MARK 10:15

What does it mean to "receive the kingdom of God like a little child"?

The disciples need to understand that they have nothing to offer God, and must therefore depend fully on God, just as a little child depends fully on its parents. Jesus is not implying that children are innocent or pure – neither of which are traits of most children!

MARK 10:38

What did Jesus mean when he said: "Can you drink the cup I drink"?

In the Old Testament, "the cup" was generally a reference to suffering. It also refers to the cup of God's anger (see Jeremiah 25:15-16). In Mark 10:38, Jesus is showing that the disciples don't know what they are talking about. They, unlike Jesus, have their own sin to deal with and therefore cannot suffer God's wrath on other people's behalf; a sinless substitute is required. However, Jesus adds – in verse 39 – that they will suffer.

MARK 11:12-14, 20-21

Why did Jesus curse the fig-tree?

This can seem strange as it is Jesus' only destructive miracle. Mark interweaves the cursing of the fig-tree with the events in the temple (Mark 11:15-19, 27-33). In the same way that Jesus curses the fig-tree for having no fruit on it, he condemns the "fruitlessness" of Israel's religion (ie: the lack of genuine worship,

the failure to recognize Jesus as the Messiah etc).

MARK 12:1

What does the story about the vineyard mean?

The vineyard was a common Old Testament symbol of Israel. In particular, this passage is very similar to Isaiah 5, where the people of Israel are rebuked for the terrible way they have rejected God, and are told that God's righteous judgment will come. Jesus' hearers would have understood that the "man" in the parable was God, that the "vineyard" was the people of God, and that the missing fruit was loyalty to the Son.

MARK 12:10

What is a capstone?

This is the most important stone; the foundation stone. Here it means that although Israel's leaders have rejected Jesus, he is still the Messiah, and will become the Saviour through dying on the cross.

MARK 12:18-27

What's the point of the strange "one bride for seven brothers" story?

In Jesus' day there were two major religious groups: the Pharisees, who believed in life after death, and the Sadducees, who said that death was the end. So the Sadducees came up with this question to trick Jesus. In his answer to them, Jesus says two things. First, there is life beyond the grave, but no married relationships in heaven. Second, he makes it clear that because God is the God of the living, and is referred to as "the God of Abraham, Isaac and Jacob", it must mean that Abraham, Isaac and Jacob are still alive!

MARK 13:14

What is "the abomination that causes desolation"?

This is an example where a passage in another Gospel helps. Luke 21:20 substitutes the words "Jerusalem being surrounded by armies", for this phrase. It refers to the occasion in AD 65 when Roman armies surrounded Jerusalem after a political uprising. After a horrific five-year war, the Roman armies entered the city, desecrated the temple, and then proceeded to pull it down and destroy the city. Jesus' words in Mark 13 came true.

MARK 13:32

Why does Jesus not know the date of his own return?

Some suggest that Jesus could not be perfect, or God, if he does not know this important fact. When Jesus was born as a man he "emptied himself" (Philippians 2:7, NASB). As a child, Jesus had to grow in wisdom, just as all human children do. He was not born with complete knowledge built in. This is one of those things which helps to verify the trustworthiness of biblical history. If someone was making up the story of Jesus Christ, he would never have left in Mark 13:33!

MARK 14:12

What are "the Feast of Unleavened Bread" and "the Passover lamb"?

God commanded the Israelites to keep the annual feasts of Passover and Unleavened Bread to remind them of how he had rescued them from slavery in Egypt (Exodus 12:14-20). Israel could only be saved from the tenth plague, the death of the firstborn, by killing a lamb, eating its roasted flesh with bitter herbs and unleavened bread, and smearing the blood on the door frames. When the angel of death saw blood on a door, he "passed over" the house and spared the firstborn (Exodus 12:1-13). The meal eaten in Mark 14:12-26 takes place at Passover. Jesus' death would be the true means of rescue from God's judgment; it would be the true Passover. This is why Jesus is sometimes referred to as the Lamb of God.

MARK 14:24

What is the "blood of the covenant"?

Passover commemorates rescue from slavery in Egypt, and from the wrath of God, by the pouring out of blood (Exodus 12:23). That rescue was followed by a covenant (an agreement made by God on behalf of his people) that was sealed by a blood sacrifice (Exodus 24:6). Jesus' sacrificial death mirrors this. He bled and died to turn God's wrath away from us, and to start a new covenant.

MARK 15:33

Was the darkness an eclipse of the sun?

Not possible. Jesus was crucified at the time of the Jewish Passover, which is always at full moon. At full moon, it is impossible to have a solar eclipse. Physically there is no adequate explanation of the darkness, other than that it is a supernatural sign at the time of mankind's darkest deed – killing the Son of God.

Why do we stop reading at Mark 16:8?

Most scholars agree that Mark's Gospel ends at chapter 16:8. The women run away terrified, not knowing what to think after being told that Jesus is risen. The ending provokes the question: are you able to see who Jesus is, why he came, and what it means to follow him?

Verses 9-20 of Mark chapter 16 appear to be attempts by later writers to add a fuller resurrection ending to Mark. However, the oldest manuscripts do not include this section, and its style and vocabulary are different from the rest of Mark. This does not mean that what is contained in this ending is made up. Most of the details also appear in the other Gospels. It just means that they were probably not in Mark's original.

Questions about Christian belief

How do you know that God exists?

- There are many philosophical and scientific arguments that you can get involved in that might show that believing in God is rational and sensible. But these arguments lead to belief in *some kind* of creator, not specifically to the God of the Bible. It is usually much better to talk about Jesus and his claim to be God.

- We know God exists because he came to earth in Jesus. This is the core of Jesus' answer to Philip's question in John 14:8-9 (it's worth looking this up and reading it if the question arises).

- "Have you ever seen God?" "No, but I might have if I'd been born at the right time. If I had been alive 2000 years ago, and living in Palestine, I could have seen God."

- Jesus claimed to be God (eg: John 5:18; 20:28-29) and his actions bore out that claim. If you'd been there, you would have seen and heard him. Check out his claims as you read through Mark and come to *Christianity Explored Universal.*

- Believing in God is not "the easy option". If he is God, then you must serve him as God.

Why should we believe what the Bible says?

- Try not to get involved in defending passages that can be interpreted in a number of different ways. The best place to start is with the reliability of what the Gospels teach about Jesus, and then go on to his teaching and claims on our lives.

- Historical evidence in the New Testament is confirmed at a number of points by non-Christian, historical writers – eg: Tacitus and Josephus – and also by archaeological evidence.

- The New Testament documents were written soon after the events they describe.

- This New Testament documentation is extensive, coming from as many as ten authors, eight of whom wrote independently of each other.

- The documents are historical in character as well as theological. They contain many verifiable details of the time and culture in which they were written.

- The text of these documents has come down to us intact from the era in which it was written.

- The writers were people who suffered and died for what they believed, and were also of very high moral standing. They believed in telling the truth. It is highly unlikely they would make up these stories, or even "imagine" them.

- The Gospels are less than complimentary to the disciples who wrote them – another sign that they were not made up.

- We have good historical reasons for trusting that what we read in the Gospels is an accurate account of what Jesus did, said and claimed for himself.

- The next step is to work out what you think of Jesus – everything else flows from that.

Don't all good people go to heaven?

- What is "good"? How "good" is good enough?

- Some of us are better than others but no one meets God's standards (see Romans 3:23).

- We are not good, because our hearts are "sin factories" (Mark 7:21-22).

- People who rely on their goodness are deluded (Mark 10:17-22). There is always more we must do. We need rescuing.

- God is after friends, not "good" rebels. The issue is whose side you are on.

- The opposite is, in fact, true. "Good" people go to hell; bad people go to heaven. Those who think they are good and rely on that will be lost. Only those who know they are lost are able to receive forgiveness and eternal life from Christ.

Why would a good God send people to hell?

- God is utterly holy and good. His character is what decides right and wrong in the universe.

- God must judge everyone. He will judge fairly and well.

- Jesus is the most loving person who ever lived, but it is he who teaches most about the reality of hell. He does so because he knows it is real, and doesn't want us to suffer the inevitable consequences of our rebellion against God.

- Heaven and hell are defined by relationship. Heaven is enjoying all the good gifts of Father God, and being with him. Hell is the absence of his blessings – friendship, love, beauty etc.

- God has judged his Son, Jesus, on the cross. He went through hell, so we don't have to!

- If we understood how holy God is, we would be asking the opposite question: how can God allow anyone into heaven?

If God forgives everything, does that mean I can do what I like?

- God's grace is utterly free. Shockingly, he will save even the worst kind of criminals you can think of.

- Jesus saved a condemned thief who died on the cross next to him!

- If we properly understand how sinful we are, and how our sins have, literally, wounded God; and if we understand how amazing it is that Jesus died for us when we don't deserve it – then we want to live in a way that pleases him.

How can we be sure that there is life after death?

- People may come up with strange stories about "out-of-body experiences" but these prove nothing, and can lead to confusion.

- The Bible says that Jesus' resurrection is the pattern for our own resurrection (eg: 1 Corinthians 15:20).

- Who do you trust for accurate information about life beyond the grave? The person who has been there and come back.

- If Jesus has been raised from the dead, then we will certainly be raised from the dead, and we must look to Jesus' teaching for answers to the questions about what life beyond death will be like.

What about other religions?

- Sincerity is not truth. People can be sincerely wrong.

- If the different religions contradict each other (which they do at several major points), they cannot all be right.

- The question really is: has God revealed himself, and if so, how? Jesus claimed to be the unique revelation of God. He claimed to be God in the flesh. Are his claims valid? If Jesus is God, the other religions are wrong.

- Jesus claims he is the only way (John 14:6).

- Religions can do many good things – provide comfort, help, social bonding etc. But they are man-made ideas about God, and generally teach that we must DO something to get right with God.

- Jesus claims that his teaching is revealed from God (John 8:28), and that his followers must abandon what they think they can *do*, and rely on what he has *done* on the cross to bring forgiveness and new life to them.

What about those who have never heard about Jesus?

- We can trust God to be just; he will judge people according to their response to what they know.

- Everyone has received some revelation, even if only from the created world (see Romans 1:18-19).

- Those who have had more revealed to them will be held more responsible (Matthew 11:20-24).

- You have heard, so you must do something about it – and leave the others to God, who will treat them fairly.

Isn't faith just a psychological crutch?

- There are different questions here, like: do I just believe because my parents were Christians? Or: do I believe because I have the need for some comfort from above? Or: do I believe because I have had this or that experience?

- If our faith is based purely on experience ("Christianity works for me"), then there is no way of arguing against this objection. It might work because it's true or because of my particular upbringing or conditioning.

- However, Christianity is based on objective historical events (the death and resurrection of Jesus), and invites people to investigate and test them.

The truth of Christianity has nothing to do with our state of mind.

- The same could be applied to any belief – including atheism! (ie: I'm an atheist because my parents were; I have a deep need to be independent; I have had no experience.) None of this helps to establish whether belief in Christianity is based on truth or error.

Why does God allow suffering?

- We can't know for sure why God allowed evil into the world.

- Much suffering is a direct result of our own sinfulness (eg: that caused by drunkenness, greed, lust, etc.).

- But some is not (see John 9:1-2).

- All suffering results from the fallen nature of our world (see Romans 8:18-25).

- God uses suffering to discipline and strengthen his children (see Hebrews 12:7-11; Romans 5:3-5).

- God also uses suffering to wake people up so that they understand that there is a judgment coming to our pain-filled world (Luke 13:1-5).

- God knows our pain. He has done something about our suffering. Jesus suffered and died so that we could be forgiven and become part of the "new creation", where there will be no suffering. Jesus' death for us is the undeniable proof that God loves us.

Hasn't science disproved Christianity?

- Most people mean: "hasn't the theory of evolution replaced creation and so disproved Christianity?" People usually are not talking about archaeology which, incidentally, backs up the Bible at almost every point.

- Start by asking what they mean by the question. They may have some specific point that needs addressing and that will require some research.

- Avoid having a technical discussion about evolution, carbon dating etc.

- Ask what conclusion they are drawing from evolution. It may be a description of how life has appeared on earth (although you may want to dispute that!). But it does not answer the bigger questions: Who produced the amazing design and order that we see in the universe? For what purpose does the universe exist?

- Did the world come into being by chance? How God made the universe is not as important as the fact that he is the one who made it.

- Steer the conversation towards talking about God's existence (see above) and towards Jesus. If Jesus is God, it puts the creation/evolution debate in a completely different perspective.

If Jesus is God's Son, how can he be God too?

- Jesus lets himself be described as the "Son of God" – a term which can mean that he is the King of God's people, but can also be a claim that he is much more.

Jesus acts in the New Testament in the way that God does in the Old Testament. He speaks as God speaks, and does things that only God can do (raises the dead, forgives sins, controls nature etc.). His words and actions show that he is making a claim to be God.

Christians do not believe that there are many Gods, and that Jesus is just one of them. Christians believe that there is one God – who is a trinity. One God, three persons – the Father, the Son and the Holy Spirit in a relationship of love and service with each other.

This is complex and hard to completely understand – but why would we expect to fully understand God anyway?

Why does God hate sex?

He doesn't. He invented it and thinks it is beautiful, wonderful and powerful.

God knows best how we work, and his pattern for sex – between a man and a woman in a committed, lifelong marriage – is the way he designed it to work best.

Sex joins people together in a way that is more than physical. If we use sex in other ways, we will inevitably damage our ability to enjoy sex in the way it was intended.

It may not appear damaging to enjoy this gift in other ways, but we must trust our Maker that it is.

Christians are hypocrites – so how can Christianity be true?

The failure of many Christians to live according to their stated beliefs does not invalidate Jesus' claims to be God.

The Bible says that Jesus alone is perfect, and it is honest about the failures and weakness of his followers. The disciples in Mark are constantly making mistakes.

Jesus taught that there will always be false teachers and fakes (Mark 13:21-22) who pretend they are Christians but who are not. This is true today.

Everyone is a hypocrite in some sense. But Jesus calls those who follow him to change and grow more like him. Don't be discouraged if you have met some Christians who are not yet perfect. They never will be this side of eternity.

Can we rely on Mark's Gospel?

WHO? WHEN? WHY?

Mark was a close friend and companion of Peter, who was one of Jesus' disciples. Peter was an "apostle" (those specifically called to witness the life, death and resurrection of Jesus). Peter wrote two letters to the first-century Christian churches. In one of them he said: *"I will make every effort to see that after my departure* (ie: his death) *you will always be able to remember these things."* (2 Peter 1:15). Peter was referring to the things he saw and knew about Jesus. He passed them on to others like Mark. Peter died in the mid 60s AD. The evidence suggests that Mark wrote his Gospel around that period.

No doubt Mark was influenced by Peter's desire for the news about Jesus to be told to others in later generations, so he wrote it down in a book. His opening sentence reveals the subject of his book: *"The beginning of the gospel about Jesus Christ, the Son of God."* (Mark 1:1).

Jesus died, rose again and returned to heaven around AD30. Mark wrote about 30 years later – well within the lifetime of those who lived through the events he recorded. So Mark had to write accurately. Any inconsistencies between what people saw and what he wrote would have discredited him.

HAS MARK'S BOOK CHANGED OVER TIME?

How different is Mark's original book from the book that we have today?

We don't have Mark's original to compare with the book we call Mark's Gospel. This is normal for ancient documents, since the original copy would have been written on material such as papyrus or parchment, which would eventually rot away.

For this reason historians assess the reliability of copies of an original by asking the following questions:

- How old are the copies?

- How much time has elapsed between the writing of the original document and the production of the copies that now exist?

■ How many copies have been found?

The table below answers these questions for three widely-trusted historical works, and compares them with the New Testament (including Mark's Gospel).

	Date of original document	Date of oldest surviving copy	Approximate time between original and oldest surviving copy	Number of ancient copies in existence today
THUCYDIDES' HISTORY OF THE PELOPONNESIAN WAR	c. 431–400 BC	AD 900 plus a few late 1st-century fragments	1,300 years	73
CAESAR'S GALLIC WAR	c. 58–50 BC	AD 825	875 years	10
TACITUS' HISTORIES AND ANNALS	c. AD 98–108	c. AD 850	750 years	2
THE WHOLE NEW TESTAMENT	AD 40–100	AD 350	310 years	14,000 (approx 5,000 Greek; 8,000 Latin; 1,000 in other languages
(MARK'S GOSPEL)	(AD 60–65)	(3rd century)	(240 years or less)	

As the table shows, the oldest surviving copies of Mark were produced 240 years after his original (a comparatively small time) and an astonishing 14,000 copies exist today. So we can have great confidence that what we read is what Mark wrote.

Acknowledgements...

This second edition of the *Christianity Explored Universal* material was edited by Tim Thornborough and Alison Mitchell, building on the original "English made easy" material, and the third edition of the full *Christianity Explored* course.

The first edition was developed by Barry Cooper, Stephen Nichols, Sam Shammas and Su Ann Woo.

Special thanks to our review panel, who have commented on this second edition of the course: Alex Bedford, Nicole Carter, Craig Dyer, Peter and Kerry Fee, Duncan Forbes, Pete Jackson, Gillian Pegler, Simon Smallwood and Anne Woodcock.

Dashing designs by Steve Devane and André Parker.

Christianity Explored Ministries (CEM) aims to provide Christian churches and organisations worldwide with resources which explain the Christian faith clearly and relevantly from the Bible. CEM receives royalties from the sale of these resources, but is reliant on donations for the majority of its income. CEM is registered for charitable purposes in both the United Kingdom and the USA.

www.ceministries.org

Keep on exploring…
www.christianityexplored.org

The *Christianity Explored* website helps non-Christians to explore Jesus' life and message in their own way and in their own time. It is equally useful for those thinking about coming on a course, and those who are going through *Christianity Explored Universal*. It features:

• a visual outline explaining the gospel message, based on the Gospel of Mark

• real-life stories from people who've become Christians

• short videos answering tough questions. These include:

> *You can't trust the Bible, can you?*
> *Hasn't science shown that Christianity is wrong?*
> *If there is a God, why does he allow suffering?*
> *Wasn't Jesus just a great teacher?*
> *Why bother with church?*
> *Isn't believing in the resurrection ridiculous?*
> *How can a loving God send anyone to hell?*
> *Why are Christians so old-fashioned about sex?*
> *Surely it's arrogant to say your religion is the only right one?*
> *Doesn't becoming a Christian mean becoming boring?*

Supporting downloads available from www.ceministries.org

■ **Bible passages** – All the passages from Mark that are studied during the course are available as downloads, with each NIV passage printed on a single sheet. These sheets may be helpful if your group members would find it difficult to work from a full Bible with small type. They may also help those with English as a second language, as there is space to add notes or translations of difficult words.

■ **Word lists** – Each study includes a list of Bible words from the session's passages. This list is printed in both the group members' Handbook and the Leader's Guide. If you would also find it helpful to have a separate printout of the list, or to project it onto the wall of your meeting room, you can download a copy from the website.

■ **Feedback forms** – You may find it helpful to use a feedback form at the end of the course, both to find out how helpful the course was and also to discover what your group members would like to do next. A sample form is available on the website in a variety of designs and sizes. There is also a feedback form that you can give to leaders to get their comments and any suggestions for improvements.

■ *Christianity Explored* **DVD trailers** – If you are going to show the *Christianity Explored* DVD during each session, then you may like to use a trailer as a way of inviting people to join. These can be downloaded from the website.

■ **Logos for your own invitations** – If you are going to create your own printed invitations to the course, you can download copies of the *Christianity Explored* logo, which is available in a number of formats.

■ **Other recommended resources** – Looking for something to help you or a course member with a particular issue? You'll find a huge range of recommendations, information and ideas on the website.

■ **Evangelistic website** – you may find it helpful also to look at *Christianity Explored's* other website, which is designed for non-Christians. This includes testimonies, video clips of answers to common questions, and an outline of the gospel message. The web address is **www.christianityexplored.org**